when you GIVE A
Lawyer
A KISS

ANN EINERSON

Paperback ISBN: 978-1-960325-09-9

Cover Design by Sarah, Okay Creations
Dev Edited by Emerald Edits, @probablyalovestory, @bookswithkaity, @bryannareads
Edited by Lyndsey Goss, @thecozy.homebody
Proofread by Britt Taylor, Paperback Proofreader
Formatted by Champagne Book Design

For anyone who feels lost, some of the most unexpected paths lead to the most unexpected surprises—like a grumpy billionaire covered in tats with a penchant for calling you 'good girl.' Hope you enjoy the ride with Dawson Tate.

PLAYLIST

Someone to You - BANNERS (feel good)
I Like the Way You Kiss Me -Artemas
Stargazing - Myles Smith
The Alchemy - Taylor Swift
Daydreaming - Harry Styles
Mr. Brightside - The Killers
August - Taylor Swift
This Town - Niall Horan
Look After You - The Fray
Kiss Me More - Doja Cat
Kiss Me - Sixpence None The Richer
Happy Little Things - Holly Kluge

AUTHOR'S NOTE

Hey, Reader!

Thank you for picking up *When You Give a Lawyer a Kiss*. It's a standalone workplace romance between a grumpy billionaire and his new assistant in an age gap, banter-filled, spicy love story.

This is a fast-paced, low drama, light and fluffy romance meant to tug at your heartstrings and have you swooning as Dawson & Reese fall in love.

While the laws and processes in this book have been researched for accuracy, some have been embellished to enhance the storyline to make you fall even harder for the grumpy billionaire.

When You Give a Lawyer a Kiss contains explicit sexual content, profanity, mention of a parent's death, and mention of absentee parents.

Reading is meant to be your happy place—choose yourself, your needs, and your happiness first!

Xoxo,

Ann Einerson

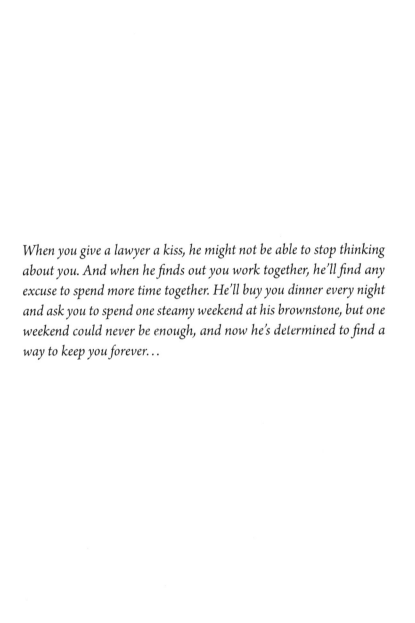

When you give a lawyer a kiss, he might not be able to stop thinking about you. And when he finds out you work together, he'll find any excuse to spend more time together. He'll buy you dinner every night and ask you to spend one steamy weekend at his brownstone, but one weekend could never be enough, and now he's determined to find a way to keep you forever...

when you GIVE A
Lawyer
A KISS

PRØLØGUE

Reese

"**Y**OU WOULD LOOK PRETTIER IF YOU PUT MORE EFFORT into your appearance. My mother thinks every woman should wear a dress, especially on a first date," Kevin says with a smug smile. "At least you're predictable, that's something I appreciate," he adds, his tone condescending.

My fingers tighten around the menu as I take a deep breath. "I'll keep your suggestion in mind," I say.

He taps his teeth together while checking his phone. "Good. Like Mother always says, a little effort goes a long way," he states, oblivious to my frustration.

He's such an asshole.

This has quickly become the worst date I've ever been on.

I set my menu down and take a sip of my water, glancing around as I weigh my chances of slipping out of the restaurant unnoticed. As if he can read my mind, Kevin squeezes my knee under the table.

With a resigned sigh, I lean back in my chair. When he first messaged me, he was charming and witty. After a month of video chats and texts, he asked me out to dinner at Tuscany Table, an Italian spot in Brooklyn. I was excited to see if our connection would be as strong in person. Spoiler alert: It isn't.

First, he dragged me to a pet store to buy crickets for his lizard—a pet he conveniently forgot to mention. He's been on his phone nonstop, likely searching for a woman who will wear a dress on a date. And he won't stop complaining about the menu prices, even though he chose the restaurant.

I can't believe I let Noah talk me into signing up for a dating app, let alone agree to meet someone I barely know.

The server approaches, a friendly smile on his face. "What can I get you two?"

I open my mouth to speak, but Kevin beats me to it. "I'll have the lasagna, and she'll take the eggplant parmesan," he says.

How would you know what I want? You haven't asked.

To keep myself from saying something I'll regret, I take another sip of water. While I would have preferred red wine, Kevin dismissed the waiter when he asked for our drink order. It's obvious Kevin is aiming to spend as little as possible since he ordered the two cheapest items on the menu.

I wish I had the courage to get up and leave. I want to tell him he's a condescending, arrogant asshole, and I'd rather be at home eating ice cream in my pajamas, watching reruns of *Love Island*, but my fear of confrontation keeps me glued to my seat to avoid causing a scene. Resigned, I hold back my sigh and slide my dinner fork farther away. I don't trust myself not to use it if Kevin puts his hand on my knee one more time; aversion to confrontation be damned.

I glance up to see the server jotting down our order. "Is there anything else I can get you?"

"That will be all," Kevin says tersely.

"Excellent; I'll be out with your food shortly." The waiter pockets his notepad and heads back to the kitchen.

I wish he'd taken me with him.

"You're going to love the eggplant parmesan," Kevin says, which prompts me to turn back to him. "It's my mother's favorite."

I plaster on a fake smile. "I'm sure I will."

It might just be me, but I find it odd that he keeps bringing up his mom. My mom passed away when I was a toddler, and while I'm close to my grandma, I would never bring her up on a first date unless it was relevant to the conversation.

When Kevin's phone chimes, he picks it up, smiling while reading the message on the screen.

"My mom wants to meet you," he says enthusiastically.

I sputter, water spraying from my mouth. "Why? This is our first date."

Besides my best friend Noah, I've never brought a man to meet my grandma. If I were to introduce her to someone else, we'd have spent far more time together or were serious enough to warrant her approval. So, I'm struggling to understand Kevin's logic.

"We've been talking for weeks," he reminds me. "She wants to meet the woman who's captured my heart."

My spine stiffens and I blink rapidly as his words sink in. "Hold on. Have you been sharing our conversations with your mom?"

He nods enthusiastically. "Of course. She's especially grateful for the play-by-play since she couldn't be here with us. We'll have to bring her with us on our next date."

Alarms blare in my head. We are definitely not on the same page.

I have to get out of here.

My pulse is racing, and my palms are clammy. I set my glass on the table, pushing my chair back and stand up quickly. "Excuse me, I need to visit the restroom," I blurt out, barely able to contain my panic.

Without waiting for him to answer, I grab my purse from the

table and hurry toward the back of the restaurant. I see the signs leading to the hallway with the restrooms but hesitate when I spot a door that opens onto an outdoor patio.

"That's not the way to the bathroom." Kevin's voice cuts through the air.

I glance back to see that he's following me, his face twisted with anger. Instinctively, I sprint toward the exit. Once outside, I weave through the tables as I evade curious looks from other patrons and turn into a narrow alley next to the building.

"Reese, stop running," Kevin shouts from behind me. "You owe me an explanation."

Like hell I do.

The stifling humidity wraps around me like a damp blanket, and when I exit the alley, sweat is dotting my forehead—I'm unsure if it's from the heat or my nerves. My jeans and short-sleeve shirt offer little relief in the muggy summer air. My body trembles from the adrenaline, my heartbeat racing, and my breaths coming out in short, ragged bursts.

I frantically scan for a place to hide before Kevin catches up with me. Both the bakery next door and the clothing boutique across from the restaurant are closed. Just when I'm about to lose hope, I spot Steel & Ink, a tattoo parlor with its lights still on a few doors down. Kevin is still in the alley, so I dart inside, sighing in relief when the bell chimes.

As soon as the door closes behind me, I lean against it and let out a long breath. The most exercise I get is walking around the city, so running away from a disastrous date is more than I bargained for.

Once I've regained my composure, I survey the shop. Four tattoo stations are on the left, each separated by solid black wooden panels and heavy doors for privacy. On the right, there's a large reception area with leather chairs and polished end tables stacked with magazines. My gaze shifts to the reception desk, and I frown when I see it's unoccupied.

The shop appears empty, and I can't afford to wait around and risk Kevin seeing me through the front window. I notice the door to the first tattoo station is open, so I duck inside.

One thing is for sure, I'm deleting my dating profile as soon as I get home. I might even swear off men altogether after this. All I've met are a series of disappointments in my limited experience, and it doesn't seem worth the effort.

"We're closed," a deep male voice says sharply.

A startled yelp escapes me as my eyes dart to a man perched on a stool, pencil poised above a sketch pad in his lap. I was so preoccupied with escaping Kevin that I didn't notice him.

He places his things on his workstation and rises to his full height. As he steps toward me, my jaw drops.

I've never seen a man this strikingly handsome before. He looks to be in his thirties and is dressed in slacks and a white dress shirt. He has a chiseled jawline, high cheekbones, and a straight, aristocratic nose. When he runs his hands through his black hair that's styled in a crew cut, I notice that his shirt sleeves are rolled up and reveal an intricate array of black tattoos that snake up his muscular forearms, the ink contrasting with the powerful lines of his physique.

The stranger's lips form a thin line, and his piercing blue gaze remains pinned on me as he observes me up close. His eyes narrow in suspicion when he notices my trembling hands and flushed cheeks.

"Did you hear me?" My head snaps back to meet his icy stare. "I said we're closed."

I swallow hard, my mouth dry, as I nod. "I'm sorry for barging in. My date didn't go as expected, and I had to make a quick escape. He didn't take kindly to being ditched and chased after me. Your shop was the only place that had the lights on, and the door was unlocked. I figured I'd hide here until he gave up looking for me." I snap my mouth shut when I realize I'm rambling.

The stranger furrows his brows. "Did he hurt you?"

I shake my head. "It's just been a while since I was on a first date, but I don't think constantly talking about your mom is what it should look like. Meeting Mr. Right in New York City is like finding a needle in a haystack—most of the good ones are taken, and the rest avoid commitment or are workaholics." My eyebrows knit in confusion when a smirk crosses the stranger's face. "To be fair, he did take me to a nice restaurant—Tuscany Table."

"They have great mushroom risotto," he says.

"I wouldn't know," I mumble. "My date was on his phone the whole way to the restaurant. He made us stop at the pet store to buy a bag of crickets for his pet lizard and insisted on bringing them with us to dinner." I cringe at the memory of the waiter's expression when the bag started to rustle under the table. "Then he ordered for me without asking what I wanted, and the last straw was when he said he suggested his mom join us on our next date. At least I had the good sense to take my purse with me." I hold it up proudly.

The attractive stranger glares at me, and I mentally chastise myself for rambling again. It's a habit I fall into when I'm nervous.

"What's your name?" he asks.

"Reese Taylor. What's yours?"

I chide myself for disclosing my full name to someone I've just met. For all I know, he could be a con artist, gathering my information as we speak.

"Cole," he grunts. "Here's a suggestion. Next time you don't like a guy, tell him to fuck off and leave."

My mouth drops open at his brashness, caught off guard by his unfiltered comment.

"You really need to work on your bedside manner," I observe.

"It's a good thing I'm not a doctor, isn't it?" he remarks. "My clientele isn't bothered by my bluntness or colorful language."

"Well, not everyone is used to—" I break off when the bell on the front door chimes.

"Hello, anybody here?" Kevin's nasally voice drifts through the shop.

My eyes fly to Cole and I silently plead with him to let me stay. He may not have given me a warm welcome, but I can sense a flicker of empathy behind his stern demeanor. I'm holding my breath, praying for a miracle, when he wordlessly brushes past me.

"We're closed," I hear Cole snaps.

Unable to resist, I cautiously glance around the doorframe, careful not to stick my head out too far.

Kevin sheepishly rubs the back of his neck. "I seem to have lost my date. Did a redhead come in here a minute ago, by any chance?"

Cole waves around the empty shop. "Does it look like I have company?"

Kevin shifts from one foot to the other. "No."

"Well, there's your answer. And a word of advice… If a woman ditches you, it's because you were a shitty date."

"Excuse me?"

"You heard me. When a woman bails, it means she noticed a red flag or in your case, several. Stalking her isn't doing you any favors," Cole states, nodding toward the door. "Now get the hell out of my shop."

I flinch even though his words aren't directed at me. We just met, and I already know he's the last person I'd want to cross.

Kevin pulls out his cell and fumbles with the door handle. "Mother, you will never believe what just happened to me…" His voice trails off as he disappears into the night.

Why am I not surprised his mom is the first person he called?

7

I let out a sigh and watch as Cole flips the sign in the window to *Closed*.

"Your date's gone. You can come out now," he calls over his shoulder.

I hesitantly step out of his workstation and into the reception area. "Thanks for getting rid of him," I say as I push my hair back from my face.

"What did you see in that asshole anyway?" he asks bluntly. "His grating voice and receding hairline should have been enough to show he wasn't worth the effort." He dims the lights, likely to deter any other unexpected visitors from dropping in.

I put my hand on my hip. "Haven't you heard the expression about not judging a book by its cover?"

Cole scoffs. "Yeah, it's bullshit. First impressions are always spot on." He takes a container of disinfectant wipes from the counter and wipes down the reception desk. "If you had been less worried about hurting Kevin's feelings and listened to your gut instincts, you could have avoided your disastrous date."

"What about you? What would I find if I judged you by your cover?"

Cole tilts his head in my direction. "I'm a skeptic who values business above all else and I have a reputation for making grown men cry." He tosses the wipe he was using into the trash.

"You're a real ray of sunshine, aren't you?" I quip.

Why do I keep provoking the grumpy tattoo artist?

Apparently, self-preservation isn't in my playbook tonight.

"My customers come here for tattoos, not to chit-chat," Cole grunts.

I nod as I wander to the wall where several tattoo designs are hung up, all in black ink. One is a wolf, its fur rendered with fine linework to create a realistic texture. The next piece features a series of interconnected geometric shapes that create an optical illusion, some of the forms appearing to jump off the wall. Next to it, there's a striking floral skull; the rose petals are drawn with a lace-like delicacy, contrasting with the bold outline of the skull.

These are more than just tattoos—they're works of art that command attention.

"Did you design these?" I ask, waving toward the wall.

My fingers hover over the image of the wolf, they graze the glass and trace the delicate linework of its fur, in awe of the intricate details. Cole is an enigma, and I'm fascinated by how he can be so unapologetically outspoken, even abrasive, yet still possess an uncanny ability to create something so beautiful.

He approaches from behind, standing close enough for me to feel the heat of his body, and the scent of leather and sandalwood surrounds me.

"Yeah, I did," he says, his voice low.

I turn my head back to look at him. "You're exceptionally talented."

While I enjoy doodling simple floral designs, these are on a whole different level. Despite his gruff demeanor, Cole's art offers a glimpse into another side of him, stirring a curiosity inside me that I want to explore.

I tug my lip between my teeth as I study his work. I've never considered getting a tattoo until now, but seeing his artwork makes me curious what it would be like to get one. To feel his strong hands on me, his touch firm and confident as he marks my skin.

I'm about to shake off the idea as impractical and impulsive when Kevin's words echo in my mind.

At least you're predictable.

He might have considered it a compliment, but I didn't see it that way. I never take chances or confront things head-on, preferring to stay in my comfort zone. But what if, for one night, I was adventurous? To prove to myself I can do it. Then tomorrow, I can go back to my predictable ways, having had a taste of living on the edge.

I spin around to face Cole. "I'd like you to give me a tattoo," I declare, sounding more confident than I am.

He rears back like he's offended. "No."

"Why not? You're a tattoo artist, it's your job," I remind him. "And I'm a paying customer." I hold out my purse with false bravado.

I'm not sure what a tattoo costs, so I'm hoping the fifty dollars I set aside for new sneakers will cover it.

"For starters, we're closed." He motions to the dimly lit room.

"Oh, come on," I protest, tugging my shirt up to reveal my hip. "What about a butterfly right here?" I point to the bare skin.

Cole rolls his eyes. "A tattoo is meant to be personal and should tell a unique story. Don't shy away from choosing something that's special to you, even if it's somewhere only you can see." I swear his gaze burns hotter, but I brush it off as my mind playing tricks. "But don't be a damn sheep when it comes to permanent ink."

My eyes drift to the compass tattoo on his forearm. The detailed blackwork is a network of fine lines and shading, creating a masterful design. I can't help but wonder what the story is behind that one.

I let out a humorless chuckle. "Are you always this warm and friendly to clients?"

"Worse. Consider yourself lucky that I'm turning you away."

"You're such a jerk," I mumble under my breath.

"Looks like you're a magnet for jerks tonight, huh?" He rakes his fingers through his hair, letting out an exasperated sigh. "Where did you meet that guy anyway? He's a real piece of work."

I adjust my purse, hiking it up my shoulder, and glance at the ground. "A dating app."

Which I'm deleting asap.

"That's where you went wrong," Cole points out. "People

can pretend to be anyone online, but in real life, they rarely measure up."

I hold my finger up in challenge. "There's one problem with your theory."

He raises a brow. "Yeah, and what's that?"

I cross my arms over my chest, lifting my chin. "I met you the old-fashioned way, and you're a jerk too," I say with a smug smile.

It's strange how they share similarities yet are so different. With Kevin, I left at the earliest opportunity, but with Cole, I'm looking for any excuse to stay.

"I might be a jerk, but at least when I'm on a date, the woman has my full attention and respect." My traitorous heart beats faster as he draws closer. "If I were him, I would have taken you to a rooftop restaurant with a stunning view of the city and ordered the most expensive bottle of champagne." Cole leans in until our noses almost touch. This close, I can see the gold flecks in his eyes, how his gaze burns with intensity, but rather than feel intimidated, I'm intrigued. "And at the end of the night, I would have kissed you until neither of us could think straight," he adds in a whisper, so low I have to edge forward.

His declaration sends a flurry of butterflies through my stomach, making me wish he'd kiss me now.

He trails his finger along my arm in teasing strokes. The tension between us crackles like a live wire, making it impossible to focus on anything but him.

"Is that so?"

Cole may be abrasive and just told me to leave five minutes ago. Yet, he didn't hesitate to protect me when Kevin showed up, talked me out of getting a tattoo I'd no doubt regret come morning, and made me feel more alive than I have in ages, which is a stark contrast from my boring, predictable routine. *Is this really happening right now?*

I inhale deeply when he captures me around the waist and

pulls me against his chest, a spark of electricity coursing through me at his touch. I might be going on a dating hiatus after tonight, but there's no denying I'm attracted to this man.

"Tell me I can kiss you, Reese."

It wouldn't hurt to do something reckless for once, right? I'll probably never see Cole again, and I have a feeling he knows how to satisfy a woman.

"Yes, please," I murmur.

I'm frozen in place when he leans in to kiss along the edge of my jaw. My breathing quickens and I glance up to find his cold gaze softened, replaced by a deniable hunger that radiates desire.

Cole's mouth finds mine in a possessive kiss and his tongue dances along the seams of my lips, coaxing me to let him in. He lets out a low growl when I open my mouth and welcome him inside. He lifts me onto the reception desk, and I instinctively wrap my legs around his waist as my fingers grip the nape of his neck.

"Fuck, I knew you'd taste sweet, Red," Cole murmurs.

Emboldened by his words, I nip his bottom lip, moaning as I delve my tongue inside his mouth. I never expected a kiss to be so intense—an all-encompassing mix of passion and desire.

He rocks his hips against mine, his bulge rubbing against my core. My nipples grow achy, and I'm pulsing with need. I'm on the verge of begging for more when the rumble of a car engine outside has me pulling away. I'm met with Cole's gaze, his striking blue eyes studying me closely as if gauging my reaction. His hair is tousled from my grip, chest heaving like he's just run a marathon, and his pupils are dilated.

Oh my god.

I just kissed a stranger. What was I thinking? I wasn't—that's the problem. His good looks and blunt honesty clouded my judgment.

I've got to get out of here.

I shove at Cole's chest, causing his grip on my waist to slip, and I fall from his arms. Thankfully, I land on my feet, with a loud umph passes my lips when I hit the wood floor.

"You all right?" he asks, concern evident in his tone.

"Yep, just peachy." I bend down to pick up my purse, which I dropped on the floor during our make out session. "I have to go."

A flicker of emotion flashes across his face before he masks it with an impassive exterior. "Yeah, okay," he says as he steps back.

My cheeks flush with embarrassment. That kiss was incredible, but he doesn't seem fazed. He must do this kind of thing all the time—he has heartbreaker written all over him.

"Thanks for letting me hide out here. I really appreciate it," I tell him as I rush toward the front door. "And for the record, you're far more likable than you make yourself out to be."

He laughs dryly. "Not a single person in New York would agree with you."

"They must not know you as well as I do." I wink. "It was nice meeting you, Cole."

I bolt out the door before he can respond. As I head toward the subway, my mind buzzes from the unforgettable kiss I just shared with a tattoo artist in Brooklyn. I touch my swollen lips, etching it into my memory so I'll never forget the thrill of doing something so exhilarating and spontaneous.

CHAPTER 1

Reese

Three Months Later

ROB SPITS OUT THE BITE OF THE SCONE AS IF IT WERE spoiled. "What the hell is this?" he demands, wiping his mouth with a napkin. "I specifically asked for cranberry orange. There's no orange in this." His tone drips with disgust as he pushes the pastry aside.

He slouches back in his chair, his appearance reflecting his sour mood—thinning hair slicked back, his stomach straining against the buttons of his white shirt, and a rumpled suit that looks like it's seen better days.

"They were out so I ordered the closest thing they had," I rush to explain.

It's my first week working for Rob, and I already loathe him. Now if only I could express my frustration without risking my job.

He rolls his eyes. "Does it look like I care? Your job is to assist me, and so far, you're doing a shitty job at it." He leans over to toss the scone into the trash.

My stomach tightens as I watch him discard perfectly good food. In my rush to get to the office this morning I skipped breakfast and couldn't afford the ten-dollar pastries from the fancy bakery he sent me to. He requires that I show him the receipts to make sure I don't buy anything for myself, even though he uses a company card. His reasoning is that it's only for partners at the firm, and lowly paralegals like me aren't entitled to the same perks.

"I'll make sure to get you a cranberry orange scone next time," I assure him.

"See that you do," he snaps. "How can I trust you with confidential client files if you can't even handle a simple task like getting my breakfast order right?"

I clench my fists at my sides and bite my tongue. Fetching his breakfast isn't in the job description, but he's had it out for me since my first day when I corrected the misspelling of a client's name on an important document he asked me to file. In the past five days, he's punished me by assigning me menial errands instead of letting me do my actual job.

I might not like the guy, but the last thing I need is to get fired on my first week because I mouthed off to my new boss, especially after all the effort I put into landing this job.

For the past year, I worked as a paralegal at a small law firm on the West Side. After applying for several positions, I was elated to land an interview with Thompson & Tate, the most prestigious law firm in New York City. I knew securing a job here would significantly improve my chances of getting into law school. Not that it matters since I still need to pass the LSAT and apply. At this rate, I may never get the chance to fulfill my dream of becoming a lawyer.

Fortunately, the position at Thompson & Tate pays three dollars more per hour than I was making at my previous job. Combined with my part-time job at Echo, a lounge bar in the city, I should be able to tackle some overdue projects on the house my grandma left me when she moved into an assisted living facility and still save a sizeable amount for law school as long as I budget wisely.

Rob taps his pen against his desk as he narrows his eyes. "Why are you still here?" he demands. "Get back to work. We have an all-hands meeting at eleven, so don't be late." He turns to his computer, effectively dismissing me.

"I won't be," I promise on my way out.

When I get to my desk, I check my phone to find an unread text from Noah.

We met in our Introduction to Law class during my freshman year of college. I was running late and had to take the only available seat next to him in the front row. After being paired up for a debate, we discovered that not only did we share an aspiration to become lawyers but also our love for Sunday brunch and Hallmark movies.

> **Noah:** Hey babe.
>
> **Reese:** Hey! How was your date with Jason last night?
>
> **Noah:** I'm thinking about taking your lead and deleting all my dating apps.
>
> **Reese:** It was that bad huh?
>
> **Noah**: The worst!
>
> **Noah**: He spent the whole night flirting with the waiter. I get it, the guy was good looking but hello I was sitting right there.
>
> **Reese:** What a jerk! He clearly has no idea what he's missing.
>
> **Noah:** You might have the right idea, taking a break from finding Mr. Right. Dating is overrated

I stifle a laugh. I'll believe it when I see it. Noah is a serial romantic who's addicted to the thrill of meeting new love interests too much to quit.

Noah: How are you holding up at the office?

Reese: Four words: Thank god it's Friday.

Noah: That boss of yours still being a pain in the ass?

Reese: That's putting it mildly.

Reese: I have my first all-hands meeting later today. Wish me luck. Let's hope the rest of the staff are more friendly than he is.

Noah: I'm sure they are. You're going to crush it.

Noah: You're at the club tonight, right?

Reese: Yeah.

Noah: David asked me to pick up a shift at the bar, so I'll see you there.

Noah bartends at Echo, and I'm a server. The tips are great, and the clientele is tame compared to the chaotic nightlife scene at other clubs.

Noah: Are we still on for our study date in the morning?

Reese: Yup. You're picking up the snacks, right?

Noah: Got them on my way to work this morning.

Noah: You can crash at my place tonight so you don't have to go all the way back to Brooklyn.

Reese: I appreciate it. You're the best.

Noah: Right back at you, babe.

Reese: Have a great day!

I'd be lost without Noah. He's been my rock, and most days,

he acts like a protective big brother and is the only person I trust besides Grams.

We have a lot in common, but the one thing we disagree on is our career paths once we become lawyers. Noah is a court clerk for the New York County Supreme Court and is set on becoming a corporate lawyer. He's drawn to the financial success that comes with it, whereas I'm passionate about roles that will allow me to advocate for disadvantaged youth.

Unfortunately, becoming a lawyer requires an excessive amount of money. We're both grappling with the financial challenges of pursuing our goals. We've been there for each other throughout this journey so far and plan to take the LSAT together in January.

I stash my phone in the top drawer of my desk and sort through the assignments Rob sent me as I dive into his emails. The next couple of hours fly by, and I'm so focused on my work that when I check the clock, I'm shocked to see it's already 10:55.

"Shit," I mumble, scrambling to collect my notebook and pen as I rush down the hall.

Being late to my first all-hands meeting would be the perfect excuse for Rob to fire me, so I've got to make it on time. After waiting for the elevator for over a minute, I decide to take the stairs. By the time I reach the top floor, I'm drenched in sweat and gasping for breath. Whoever decided that looking professional included heels has never been late and had to run up multiple flights of stairs.

As I exit the stairwell a few latecomers trickle out of the elevator, and I follow them to a large conference room at the end of the hallway. It has floor-to-ceiling windows that let in a flood of natural light, and the walls are adorned with sleek, modern art. A long conference table is positioned at the center for the partners and executive team, and dozens of chairs are arranged in a semi-circle to accommodate the rest of the staff.

From his spot near the head of the table, Rob shoots me a disapproving glare. I slip into a seat in the far corner, hoping to stay out of his line of sight, and place my notebook and pen on my lap, pretending to jot something down.

A woman in a plaid pink-and-white suit sits beside me. She smiles warmly as she extends her hand. "Hi, I'm Grace Wilford. I'm Sean Huffman's paralegal. He's a senior partner."

"I'm Reese. It's nice to meet you." I say, accepting her handshake.

"I've heard so much about you already." She scoots her chair closer. "You're a legend around here."

"You must have me confused with someone else," I tell her nervously. "All I've done since I got here is get coffee, answer emails, and file paperwork."

Grace shakes her head. "Nope. It's you." She leans in, her voice dropping to a whisper. "Anyone who can get through a week of working with Rob and still have a smile on their face is a saint in my book."

My cheeks flush with embarrassment. "He's complained about me?"

She chuckles when she notices my panicked expression. "I heard him complaining about you to an associate in the break-room yesterday, but don't worry—he's like that with everyone. He might be untouchable because his uncle is the founding partner, but let me know if you ever need help dealing with him. I've got your back." She gives me a reassuring pat on the shoulder.

"Thank you, I appreciate that," I respond with a sigh of relief.

"Of course, us paralegals have to stick together."

At my previous firm, it was a cutthroat environment with everyone vying for the same bonuses and promotions. As a result, making friends was impossible. I'm glad to find that's not the case here.

"The downside of working here is the lack of eye

candy—except for the boss, who's *gorgeous*," Grace says wistfully. "I might be tempted to make a move if I wasn't engaged and the no-fraternization policy didn't exist. Although, his attitude has most of us feeling like we're walking on eggshells, and that's a deal breaker for me."

I haven't met the "boss" yet but assume she means Dawson Tate, the managing partner. I've heard whispers in the halls about his exacting standards and prickly disposition; apparently he's as ruthless as they come. There's no photo of him on the company website so I'll have to take Grace's word about him being attractive.

"That's okay." I offer a reassuring smile. "I'm not here for the eye candy anyway, so it's for the best."

After my disastrous date with Kevin three months ago, I deleted the dating app from my phone and don't plan on going on another date anytime soon.

"Well, I'm glad we met. If you need anything, just send me a message on our chat system," Grace says before she turns her attention to the front of the room as the meeting starts.

Growing up, I was a hopeless romantic. I dreamed of grand gestures and the perfect fairytale ending. However, after a painful breakup in high school and a string of disastrous first dates, like the one with Kevin, I'm questioning whether that ideal romance is a fantasy.

That hasn't stopped me from thinking about Cole, the hot tattoo artist. I shift in my seat as I recall the feel of his mouth against mine. He was the first person I'd kissed in ages, and it was the most exhilarating kiss I've ever experienced.

I've considered going back to the tattoo parlor to explain why I left, but he seemed like the kind of person who'd probably forget about me the moment I walked out the door. Which makes it even more humiliating that the moment we shared remains so vivid in my memory.

A deep, familiar voice interrupts my thoughts, and I furrow

my brow in confusion. Did I bring my daydream to life? I look up from my notepad, where I've been doodling flowers—a habit of mine when I need a distraction.

My breath hitches when I spot those unmistakable blue eyes.

Oh my god.

It's Cole. What is he doing here?

Grace leans over to whisper in my ear. "Girl, are you okay? You look like you've seen a ghost."

I swallow the lump in my throat, collecting my thoughts. "Who's that speaking?" I nod toward Cole.

"*That's* Dawson Tate. I was right about him being eye candy, huh?" Grace says with a hint of mischief.

I nod. "Uh-huh."

The last thing I want is for my new coworker to discover that I've made out with our boss. Although he wasn't officially my boss then. I doubt it would matter—I'll still be shown the door.

Grace settles back in her chair, attention on *Dawson*.

Why would he use a fake name?

He hasn't noticed me yet, and I'm too stunned to formulate a discrete exit strategy as my surroundings start to blur. I can't quite grasp that Cole from the tattoo parlor is actually Dawson Tate, managing partner at Thompson & Tate.

Maybe I can go undetected. Dawson doesn't strike me as someone who spends a lot of time with the paralegals, and we work on different floors. If I sit in the back during meetings, there's a good chance he'll never notice me.

I keep my head down, and lose myself in my thoughts as I doodle in my notepad to ease my nerves, barely registering what's being said in the meeting. By the time it wraps up, I'm practically on the edge of my seat, anxious to return to my desk.

Despite my attempts to ignore Dawson, I can't help but glance at him one more time. It's a decision I immediately regret as his gaze locks onto mine. He studies me with a hint of amusement before his face reverts to its inscrutable mask.

Before anyone can exit the conference room, Dawson clears his throat. "Reese Taylor, I'd like to see you in my office," he announces, motioning toward me. Every head in the room swivels in my direction with a combination of shock and intrigue, their whispered speculations filling the air.

It's obvious that a summons to see him means someone's in trouble. For me, it's a simple case of bad timing and my inability to control my reaction to his striking looks.

Dawson doesn't wait for my response before collecting a stack of documents from the conference table and striding out of the room, leaving me to find his office on my own.

I stand, shifting from foot to foot as I fidget with my hands. I'm almost certain I'm about to be fired. There's no chance Dawson will let me stay. It would be a nightmare for HR, considering he's the managing partner of a multibillion-dollar firm, and I'm just a paralegal.

As I muster the courage to confront the situation, I notice Rob storming toward me with a scowl on his face.

"How do you know Dawson Tate," he demands when he reaches me.

"I don't," I lie.

Dawson doesn't strike me as someone who shares his personal life with his employees, so I keep the truth to myself.

Rob's eyes narrow. "You better not embarrass me," he warns. "Dawson might be in charge, but my uncle is the founding partner. If I decided to have you terminated, you'd be gone by the end of the day." He punctuates his words with a snap of his fingers.

"I believe you." His empty threats are the least of my worries, but that doesn't stop me from trying to appease him.

"I expect a full report when you get back to your desk."

"Rob, aren't you late for meeting with the other associates?" Grace interjects, as she comes to stand next to me.

"Mind your own business," he snarls.

Grace rolls her eyes as he pushes past us, storming out of the room.

"He's such a jerk, but don't worry, he's all talk and no action," Grace says. "Are you okay?"

"I'm fine," I assure her with a smile. "Is it true Rob's uncle owns the firm?"

"Yeah, his name is Maxwell. I've worked here for three years and haven't met him once. From what I understand, he doesn't interact with clients directly. There's even a rumor going around that he was involved in a financial scandal, and Dawson reportedly had to fix it to keep the company from going under." She leans in closer and lowers her voice. "Apparently Rob resents Dawson because the firm started as a family business, and he thinks he should be a managing partner despite his lack of experience." She pauses, glancing at her watch. "You better get going. The boss doesn't like to be kept waiting."

"Where is Dawon's office?"

"At the end of the hall on the left." She points, motioning in the general direction. "Good luck."

"Thanks," I say, heading out of the conference room.

My heart pounds with every step closer I get to Dawson's office. I swallow thickly when I arrive, staring at the closed door while gathering the courage to knock. After three tentative taps, his voice filters through from the other side. "Come in."

When I open the door, I find him sitting at his desk, focused on his laptop, his fingers flying across the keys.

"You asked to see me?" I say, feigning confidence.

"Shut the door," Dawson orders.

My hands tremble as I obey, the click echoing throughout the office as the door latches. Despite the urge to cower under his intimidating gaze, I straighten my spine and purposefully stride toward him, stopping in front of his desk.

The room is spacious, with rich mahogany bookshelves holding an extensive collection of legal volumes. Across the room, a leather couch sits beneath a piece of contemporary art, and a well-stocked bar cart is positioned in the corner. Large windows provide a sweeping view of the bustling city below.

Dawson rises from his leather chair, coming to stand in front of me. My earlier confidence evaporates from being in the same space as New York's most feared lawyer.

I'm a skeptic who values business above all else and I have a reputation for making grown men cry.

Now I see that Dawson's words from the night we met had a double-meaning. I assumed he was talking about his work as a tattoo artist, but it's clear now he was referencing in part his ability to make the toughest men to tears during negotiations.

As the air between us thrums with an invisible energy, my skin prickles with anticipation. I square my shoulders and meet his gaze with an unwavering resolve, readying for whatever comes next.

CHAPTER 2

Dawson

THE SWEET SCENT OF COCONUT AND PINEAPPLE FILLS THE air, causing me to clench my jaw. It's the same one that's plagued my memory for the past three months.

I'm known for my ironclad control. It's one of the reasons I'm such a damn good lawyer. I'm willing to wait out my opponent until they fold like a house of cards. In my line of work, being caught off guard means losing the case, translating into millions of dollars in losses.

Which means I'm *always* prepared for anything.

Until now.

The one thing I hadn't planned for was showing up to the all-hands meeting today and seeing Reese, the quirky and chatty woman from the tattoo parlor that I haven't stopped thinking about.

"What are you doing here?" I ask sharply. "Did you know this was my firm?"

I pulled up her employee file while I waited for her to get here. This is her first week, but she applied once before earlier this year, which admittedly sets her apart in an industry where that kind of tenacity is rare. Her persistence is impressive and shows a determination that most don't possess. I also found several glowing reports from her previous law firm, which praised her as an outstanding employee with an exceptional work ethic. Still, I'm skeptical of her motives. I can't help but wonder if she intentionally showed up at Steel & Ink before securing a job at my company as a larger scheme to expose my secret. It seems far-fetched, but I'm not ready to dismiss the possibility yet.

Reese shakes her head. "How would I have known? You told me your name was Cole."

She has a good point.

I pinch the bridge of my nose. "That's my middle name."

Adopting an alias at the tattoo shop helps keep that part of my life separate from my law career.

"That would have been nice to know before," she mumbles mostly to herself.

"Tell me, Reese, why did you want to work here?"

"Because it's the best firm in the city." She fidgets with her hands, glancing down at the ground.

While she speaks, my eyes wander to her black A-line skirt, which falls just below her knees, accentuating her curves. Her red hair frames her heart-shaped face, loose waves fall around her shoulders, and images of me gripping it tightly while I plant an electric kiss on her lips infiltrate my mind.

That's an inappropriate thought to have about my employee.

I rationalize the fleeting thought by reminding myself that she didn't work for me when we shared a kiss a few months back.

I run my fingers through my hair, shifting my gaze to the window. "No one at the office knows that I own a tattoo shop, and I'd like to keep it that way, understand?" I say, my tone firm.

A tattoo artist doesn't exactly match the polished image my clients expect when they're paying top dollar for a lawyer. There's a reason I've gone out of my way to keep my tattoos hidden and project the kind of persona that's fitting for a prestigious attorney.

"If you're trying to fly under the radar at your tattoo parlor, the slacks and dress shirt aren't doing you any favors." Reese claps her hand over her mouth, looking just as surprised as I am that she said that out loud.

I resist the urge to smile. She's in the lion's den, but doesn't shy away from calling me out. That's something I respect. I use the moment to look at her more closely. Her green eyes, bright as emeralds, shine with a quiet intensity and are framed by a nose dusted with freckles.

God, she's more beautiful than I remember.

And off-limits, I remind myself.

"I usually go straight to Steel & Ink after work on Fridays, and no one cares what I wear, so there's no reason to change."

"So it's like the luxury version of a secret hobby? Some people do subversive cross-stitch. Others brew their own beer in basements. Rich law firm partners buy and operate tattoo parlors. Got it."

I clear my throat. "By all means, Ms. Taylor, tell me what you really think," I say dryly. "Do you always make it a habit of speaking your mind?"

"Only when I'm feeling particularly inspired." Reese's cheeks flush pink as she smooths out her skirt. "Are you going to fire me?" she blurts out.

Her question causes me to pause. I'm good at gauging someone's true intentions, and I believe she's telling the truth about applying to work here, unaware that I was the managing partner.

I watch her closely. "I'm not going to fire you."

She gives me a skeptical glance. "You're not?"

"No."

An idea quickly takes shape in my mind, and against my better judgment, I run with it. "But I am going to assign you to my team. My paralegal quit last month, and I've just taken on a high-profile case that needs additional support," I say as the ghost of a smile crosses my face before composing my expression.

What the hell am I doing?

The paperwork alone to transfer her would be a nightmare, but that's HR's problem. If I were smart, I'd send her on her way and avoid the second floor for as long as she's here. When checking her file, I couldn't help but notice that she's only twenty-three. Far too young for a thirty-five-year-old skeptic who bends the rules when it suits me; my moral compass is often skewed when seeking justice.

The last thing I need is to spend more time near the stunning woman who brings out a side of me I prefer to keep hidden.

"You can't have me transferred," Reese protests, her voice edged with panic.

I cock my head to one side, taken aback by her frantic plea. "Why not? I'm the managing partner of this firm, and I can make decisions regarding my employees, including onboarding staff members."

She glances at the door like she's ready to bolt. "What happened at the tattoo parlor was a mistake, and I'd really like to pretend it never happened."

What the hell?

I blink rapidly, unsure if I heard her correctly. I've never had a woman suggest she regretted kissing me. They're usually begging for more before our night together ends. And it stings that she'd assume I would ask her to join my team as leverage to manipulate a physical relationship.

If Reese were ever in my bed, it's because she wanted to be there. But she's made it clear she's not interested, and I've had to remind myself for the second time that she's strictly off-limits.

I put my hand over my heart in a dramatic fashion. "I'm wounded."

"Something tells me your ego can afford the hit," she retorts.

I swallow hard. "Rest assured, I'm asking you to work with me in a strictly professional capacity."

Although it's the truth, I'm silently cursing the non-fraternization policy. Why is it that the only woman I've been interested in sleeping with in ages is the one I can't have?

"Is your objection working directly with me?" I ask.

She nods. "I was hired as Rob's paralegal. The gossip would spread if you transferred me after only a week on the job, and I'd rather avoid that. I want to earn my place here on my own merit, not because I have an in with the boss."

I roll my eyes at the mention of Rob. That clown thinks he's untouchable because he's Maxwell's nephew, but he's just as expendable as the rest of our employees. If it weren't for me, this place would have gone under when Maxwell was exposed for embezzling client funds. Thanks to my ability to think on my feet—and my talent for spinning stories—the company's reputation remained unscathed, and I became a managing partner.

"Rob will be fine without you," I say, waving off her concern.

He's a junior partner with a limited portfolio and isn't assigned high-profile cases requiring extra resources. I'm not sure why HR approved his request for a paralegal in the first place.

"As for the gossip, no one will question my decision, trust me." I might not be able to squash every piece of gossip, but I'll damn well do my best if it means she'll agree.

Reese straightens her shoulders and lifts her chin to meet my gaze. "Mr. Tate, I appreciate the offer but respectfully decline."

I move closer, our feet nearly touching, but she doesn't flinch. "And what if I don't accept your answer?"

She draws in a deep breath. "Then you'll be sorely disappointed because I'm not changing my mind."

"We'll see about that," I say, a faint smirk playing at the corners of my mouth.

She exhales sharply through her nose and narrows her eyes, clearly not amused. I've never had an employee dare question my authority until now.

She stands her ground, her steady and unyielding gaze fixed squarely on me. Anyone else would scramble to make a quick exit, but not Reese. There's something oddly compelling about her determination to challenge me, and I find myself mesmerized by her boldness.

When a stray lock of hair falls across her face, I tuck it behind her ear. She shivers at my touch, and goosebumps scatter across her arms. The charged energy between us thickens as her eyes wander to my lips. Her breathing quickens as she tilts her head toward me.

The memory of her legs clinging to my waist, her fingers tangled in my hair as she drew me closer, and the feel of her soft lips pressed against mine has me suppressing a low groan. My hands twitch at my sides, itching to grip the nape of her neck and draw her in.

Reese looks like she's battling a similar storm of emotions, her lips slightly parted as if on the verge of surrender.

The sound of voices in the hallway snaps out of my trance, and I take several steps back. What just happened between us isn't acceptable workplace conduct, and as much as I wish otherwise, it can't happen again.

In an attempt to get a handle on the situation, I clear my throat before rounding my desk to my office chair.

"You're dismissed," I tell Reese.

I catch a fleeting glimpse of her dejected expression before it vanishes.

"Yes, sir," she says with a hint of sarcasm before slipping out the door.

I massage my temples, struggling to push Reese out of my

mind. To quiet the thought that makes me want to chase after her—to hear her voice again.

Against my better judgment, I've made up my mind: I want her on my team. I can't stand the idea of her working at my firm and not seeing her every day. I'll just have to think outside the box to make it work, and I'm more than ready for the challenge.

CHAPTER 3

Reese

HEAT BLOOMS IN MY BELLY AS I THINK BACK TO MY interaction with Dawson yesterday. I could hardly concentrate on anything other than the spark of his touch. His hand caressing my cheek felt so right, my body completely ignoring the fact that he's my boss. It was like it was acting on its own, overriding the professional lines we were crossing.

I recall how close he was, how his breath warmed my skin and his lips set in a hard line. His eyes flickered with a mix of desire and restraint as if battling the urge to close the remaining distance or walk away.

Dawson offered me a way out of working with Rob, but I couldn't accept it. I was hired for a specific role and want to avoid any appearance of favoritism. This job is my primary income and supports my current expenses while I also save for law school, and I can't jeopardize that.

Not to mention if I worked closely with Dawson every day, I would be too tempted to overstep boundaries I might not be able to reverse. I'd like to think I'd be able to keep things professional, but based on my reaction yesterday, it's best not to play with fire.

I've concluded that his eagerness to have me work with him must be to keep tabs on me and protect the secret that he leads a double life. But I'd never betray him, and after seeing his incredible artwork—it's clear he has remarkable talent.

Based on his reaction, I can tell that Dawson Tate isn't used to compromising or being told *no*. He manages the most prestigious law firm in the state and from what I've heard, has a talent for bending people's will to match his own, consequences be damned.

If I have any self-preservation, I would steer clear of him at all costs.

If only that were possible.

"Reese, are you all right? Did you hear what I said?"

"Huh?" I glance over at Noah, who's staring at me from across the table with a concerned expression on his face.

He sets his textbook down to give me his full attention. "I asked what the logical flaw was with my argument, but your mind must have been somewhere else."

My face flushes at being caught daydreaming during our study session. "I'm sorry, Noah. I was thinking about Thompson & Tate."

He offers me a sympathetic smile. "Don't be. You had a tough first week, and after a long night at the club, I'm surprised you're even awake right now."

We walked back to his place after our shift last night, and I crashed on his couch. Even though we didn't get much sleep, we woke up early to study. We're both committed to scoring well on the LSAT our first try, which means taking advantage of every study session and practice test we can fit in.

"How was your first all-hands meeting? We didn't get a chance to talk about it last night."

I bury my face in my hands, to try to hide my embarrassment.

"I met Dawson Tate, the managing partner. He asked to speak with me privately in front of everyone. It was so embarrassing." I leave out the part where Dawson and Cole are the same person. I'd never hear the end of it.

Noah's pencil slips from his hand, his mouth gaping open. "You're kidding me. What the hell did you do to deserve that?"

I sigh in exasperation. "You make it sound like I was sent to see the principal."

"You're joking, right? Dawson Tate is infamous. He's merciless and never loses a case. In fact, most of his cases are settled outside of court because he's such a master negotiator." He bends to retrieve his pencil from the kitchen floor. "There's even a rumor that he's served time in prison. Whether it's true or not, it makes him more intimidating."

"He wouldn't be able to practice law if that were true." I point out.

Thoughts of Dawson's tattooed arms and his abrasive behavior make me wonder if there could be truth to the rumor. More importantly, why does the idea of him having served time make him more appealing?

Noah snickers. "Given his track record, I doubt a pesky prison sentence would deter him from doing anything."

"Probably not," I agree. "Regardless, he asked me to be his paralegal."

More like demanded.

Noah lets out a whistle. "Damn, Reese. That's impressive. I've heard that he only surrounds himself with the best."

I shift in my seat as I chew on my lower lip. "I turned him down," I confess.

Even though I'm confident I made the right choice, a shadow of doubt lingers in my mind.

"Hold up." Noah holds out his hand. "Let me get this straight. You told *the* Dawson Tate no? The man who dismantled Victor

Mangum's multibillion-dollar patent claim and made him cry at a televised civil trial, which also happened to ruin his reputation in the tech world? Why would you do that?" He stares at me with a look of disbelief.

I've been asking myself the same question. It was a reckless move, but I couldn't let him steamroll me, no matter who he is.

"Because I already have a job."

"With a boss you can't stand," Noah reminds me.

"And you think Dawson would be any better than Rob?"

He sighs. "That's a fair point. Just be careful, okay?" He reaches over to give my hand a gentle squeeze. "Dawson is older, more experienced, and has a reputation for being unyielding."

If he's so ruthless, why didn't he have an outburst when I showed up uninvited to his tattoo shop? Granted, he was less than amused, but when he talked to me he lacked the bite in his tone that he had when he confronted Kevin. And his kiss might have been rough, but it sent a shiver down my spine that left me craving more.

It's intriguing to think about why a high-powered lawyer with a hard-nosed persona spends his weekends as a tattoo artist. How can someone who draws beautiful, whimsical, imaginative tattoos make grown men cry in court?

Dawson is a puzzle I can't seem to solve, and the urge to learn more about him is only intensifying. I shift my gaze to Noah, who's watching me intently. "Are we going to spend the time we have left talking about my work or studying?"

He taps his chin, a teasing smile on his lips. "It depends. Are you going to pay attention?"

"Only if we can dig into those chicken tenders you bought."

Noah chuckles. "You got it."

As I settle my textbook into my lap, his warning lingers, but my curiosity about Dawson only grows. His enigmatic nature draws me in, and I sense there's more to him than meets the eye.

Luckily, I should be able to steer clear of him at the office and stay on top of my priorities.

The house feels like an icebox when I get home later that night. I shiver as I hurry to my bedroom and throw on a sweater, fuzzy socks, and some fingerless gloves Grams knitted me for Christmas last year.

After the pilot light went out on the furnace last month, the heating technician told me I needed to replace it, which would set me back six thousand dollars. Since the furnace supplies the hot water too, I've had to make do with cold showers.

I climb into bed and huddle under a mountain of blankets, trying to ward off the chill. It's autumn in New York and the weather has taken a turn. I shudder at the idea of going through a brutal winter without a functioning furnace.

One problem at a time, Reese.

I grab my old, battered laptop from the nightstand. Its surface is covered in scratches and dents, the screen flickers, the keys are worn, and most of the letters are rubbed off. During my freshman year of college, I found the thing in the bottom of a bin at a local thrift store and was pleasantly surprised when it actually worked. It's been my trusty sidekick ever since.

Once it's powered up, I check my bank account and sigh in relief when I see I'm not in the red. Between my monthly expenses, and the portion of Gram's senior living costs not covered by her pension or Social Security, every dollar counts. Home repairs might as well be a luxury.

In addition to the furnace being out of commission, there are rotting floorboards in my grandparents' old room, a minor mold issue in the bathroom, and a leak in the roof that causes trouble when it rains.

The house is a money pit, but I refuse to give it up. Grandpa bought it for Grams when they were newlyweds, full of dreams for their future together. He passed away from a heart attack when I was a teenager, and it would crush Grams to sell the house they lived in together for over forty years. Not to mention I've spent my whole life here, and the thought of moving is heartbreaking.

It's also where my mom grew up, and I feel connected to her living here. She was an only child who excelled in everything she did—captain of the cheer squad, valedictorian, and full-ride college scholarship. When she came home to visit during her junior year of college pregnant, my grandparents were shocked but supportive. She never mentioned a man before, only that he was older and had no interest in being a father.

When I was a toddler, my mom was diagnosed with stage four Hodgkin lymphoma—a type of blood cancer. She passed away six months later. In preparation of her death, she documented every milestone, wrote me dozens of letters, and filled several albums with photos of us together to leave me physical reminders of her love. With no solid memories of my mom, these keepsakes are a lifeline, offering comfort and easing the pain of her absence.

I'm about to close my laptop when temptation gets the better of me. My fingers fly across the keyboard and soon, I'm scrolling through endless search results for Dawson.

He completed his undergraduate degree in New York and attended Yale Law School. He accepted a job offer at Thompson & Tate shortly after and quickly climbed the ranks to become the firm's youngest partner. There are dozens of articles about his cutthroat reputation and how he's become one of the most sought-after corporate attorneys in the country. Some reports even suggest that his strategic investments have made him a billionaire, and his financial empire extends beyond his law practice.

In stark contrast, the tattoo artist I met three months ago has a talent for transforming ink into vibrant life and proudly shows off his own tattoos instead of hiding them under long-sleeved dress shirts. That man didn't appear driven by the relentless pursuit of success or financial gain. It raises the question, which side of him is the authentic one—the ambitious lawyer or the artist who finds fulfillment in self-expression?

After tossing and turning all night, I take the subway to visit my grandma at Oak Ridge, the assisted living facility where she moved five years ago after she slipped and fell on a patch of ice. Her recovery was long following her hip surgery, and despite my offer to postpone going to college to help her, she was insistent on moving somewhere she could receive the care she needs while maintaining a sense of independence.

When I walk inside, I'm greeted by April, an enthusiastic fifty-year-old brunette wearing a woolen, sapphire-colored sweater. She's sitting behind the reception desk, which is covered in posters advertising everything from puppy therapy to senior salsa classes.

She gives me a warm smile. "Hey, Reese. How are you doing?"

"It's been a long week. I started my new job, which is exciting but also overwhelming. I'm still trying to figure out the coffee machine, keep everyone's names straight, and my boss sends me on a wild goose chase for a pastry every morning." I chuckle awkwardly, realizing I might be oversharing. "These are for the staff." I hand her the box of assorted freshly baked donuts I picked up on my way here.

I'll have to cut a few non-essentials from my grocery list this week to balance it out—including pumpkin spice coffee creamer—but it's worth it to show my appreciation for the staff. They've been so good to Grams and deserve to be recognized.

April places her hand on her heart. "That's so kind of you; you're always so generous." She places the donuts behind the reception center, out of view of the residents. "Georgia is waiting for you in the sunroom."

"Thank you," I say, giving her a wave goodbye.

When I reach the sunroom, I find Grams sitting in a rocking chair by the window, reading. Her gray hair is styled into a bob that frames her face, and she's wearing her favorite lavender cashmere sweater and matching skirt. She glances up from her book, a smile lighting her face when she sees me.

"Reese, darling. I'm so happy to see you." She smiles.

I lean down to kiss her on the cheek, inhaling the comforting scent of peppermint and cinnamon. It brings me back to my childhood of early mornings spent in the kitchen helping make her famous cinnamon rolls, Ella Fitzgerald's voice crooning in the background on my grandparents' record player.

"Hey, Grams."

She gives my hand an affectionate squeeze. "I missed you, sweet girl."

"Missed you too."

More than I can express.

A heavy weight settles on my chest. Only seeing her once a week is a bittersweet reminder that until five years ago, she lived at the house with me. She and Grandpa raised me, shaping me into the person I am today. Her absence at the house feels like a void that only deepens with each passing week.

I'm so blessed that my grandparents stepped in to raise me after my mom passed. It didn't matter that they were approaching retirement or that it added to their financial strain. They did everything to make sure I grew up in a supportive and stable environment, and I'll forever be grateful. My life could have turned out very different if they hadn't taken me in.

I'm one of the lucky ones, and I know not every kid gets the second chance I did, which is why I want to be a child advocacy lawyer.

Grams rests her hand over mine, drawing me into the present.

"How's the new job going, sweetheart? Have you made any friends?"

"It's going well. Grace, another paralegal at the firm seems really nice, but I've been so busy and haven't had much chance to get to know her yet."

"I'm glad to hear it," she smiles. "How's Noah? He hasn't been here in a few weeks."

"Great. He loves his clerkship, and we're still studying for the LSAT together every Saturday."

He's joined me on several visits, and Grams adores him. When she first met him, she tried playing matchmaker, but that quickly took a turn when she found out Noah only dates men.

"Don't wear yourself out," Grams scolds. "You're young and beautiful and should have a life outside of your job."

I force a feeble smile as my throat tightens. She's not aware that I work at Echo, nor does she know about the ever-growing list of repairs needed around the house. The last thing I want is for her to worry about me more than she already does.

"Don't worry, Grams, I won't." I tighten my hold on her hand, trying to convey that everything is okay. "I love you so much."

She tucks a lock of hair behind my ear and beams at me. "I love you too, my sweet girl."

Grams is my reason for overcoming every challenge, and someday, she'll be there cheering me on when I finally get my law degree. The sacrifices we've made will have been worth it. I won't let her down; it's not an option.

CHAPTER 4

Reese

W HEN MONDAY MORNING ROLLS AROUND, I GROAN AT
my blaring alarm and drag myself out of bed.

After visiting Grams yesterday, I spent the afternoon studying at the library since it was cold and they have heating. On my way home, I stopped by the grocery store to make the
most of their Sunday afternoon markdowns and once I made it
to my house, I curled up in bed and caught up on the latest season of *Love Island*.

I might not lead an adventurous life, but it's mine. One day,
after I've finished law school and landed my dream job, I'll look
back and see it was all worthwhile.

On my way to work, Rob sent me his breakfast order—a cappuccino and a cheese Danish from a bakery on the opposite side
of town. Of course when I got there, they'd sold out, so I had to
go to a different location.

I'm convinced he deliberately asks for a different pastry every
day and bribes the bakery into hiding their stock, making me
search multiple places for the right one. The fact that the bakeries

he sends me to are almost always out of the pastry he asks for seems to be more than just a coincidence.

When I finally reach the office, I'm late and out of breath. My phone pings in the elevator, and I take it from my purse with my free hand.

> **Noah:** Have a great day at work. If Rob gives you a hard time, tell him to suck it.

> **Reese:** I'll be sure to pencil that in between the department meeting at 9 am and the settlement agreement at 10.

> **Noah:** Heard anything from the big boss?

> **Reese:** I just got here, but I'm sure he's already forgotten about me.

> **Noah:** Somehow, I doubt that. I'm heading into the courtroom now.

> **Reese:** Okay, good luck in there. Talk soon!

I place my phone in my desk drawer when Rob pokes his head out of his office.

"Reese, get in here, now," he barks. "And bring my breakfast with you. I'm starving."

His voice carries across the open floor plan, with desks spread across the space and offices lining the perimeter. Several heads turn, curious about the commotion.

"Coming." I grab his coffee and the cheese Danish and rush into his office.

Rob stands at the door, tapping his foot impatiently, and I move past him inside and place his breakfast on the desk.

"What can I do for you?" I ask, the words feeling like sandpaper on my tongue.

He eyes me warily as he takes a seat in his leather chair. "I've been assigned to the Irving case. Since it's high-stakes and he's one of our longest-standing clients, all the other associates wanted to work on it, but I'm the one who got it," he brags as he takes a big bite of his Danish.

He has a glob of pastry filling smeared on his face, but I say nothing.

Instead, I force a smile and say, "That's great news."

High-stakes cases are considered the golden ticket for paralegals. The increased workload provides the chance to gain valuable experience, however, I doubt Rob will let me do much more than run errands and file paperwork.

"Hardly," Rob mutters through another mouthful. "It means I'm stuck working with Dawson. It's not fair that he keeps the best cases for himself. Chances are, he'll try to pawn off the worthless grunt work to me. At least I have you."

Which is another way of saying I'll be stuck doing all the menial tasks.

I raise my eyebrows. "Wait, Dawson is working on this case too?"

"Yeah, he's the lead counsel, but he asked me to assist. Not that it's any of your business," Rob adds, asserting his authority. "The bastard told me he wants you to split your time between him and me since his previous paralegal left last month, and according to him, he can't find anyone else suitable. Whatever the hell that means. I shouldn't be surprised, since he's an asshole. No one in the office can stand him," he mutters under his breath.

You're one to talk.

"How am I expected to divide my time?" I ask, keeping my unfiltered opinion to myself.

I'm already stretched thin and worried about how I'll be able to manage it all if I have to work longer hours at the firm.

"Dawson said he'll make the final call," Rob grumbles. "But remember, you're *my* employee. Step out of line, and you'll regret it," he threatens, jabbing a pudgy finger at me.

I resist the urge to roll my eyes, suspecting Dawson won't tolerate Rob's attempted power play.

"Understood. Will that be all for now?"

"Dawson wants to see you, but don't take too long. Those files won't sort themselves." He nods to a cart of documents in the corner.

I swallow the lump in my throat as I head toward the elevators. Why would Dawson change my job responsibilities when I told him no last week. The last thing I needed was for Rob to find another reason to resent me.

When I get to Dawson's office, the door is ajar. I don't bother knocking and head inside. He's at his desk, buried in paperwork, not bothering to look up.

"Sit."

Looks like we're skipping the social pleasantries this morning.

"Do I get a special treat if I do?" I deadpan.

I make sure to keep my smile sickly sweet, an eyebrow raised in silent reprimand.

Dawson's fingers tapping away at his laptop freeze, curling in on themselves, as his jaw clenches in what I assume is frustration.

"Take a seat. *Please.*" He motions to the chair in front of his desk. "I take it Rob shared the news?"

I lower myself into the chair and clasp my hands as my nerves attempt to stage a coup on my newly discovered courage. "I appreciate the offer from Friday, but I turned it down, remember? I'm happy to assist Rob with his part of the Irving case, but it's best if you and I keep our distance. There are plenty of other paralegals in the firm you can assign to work with you directly." I mentally give myself a high-five for standing my ground.

Dawson looks up from his computer, his piercing blue eye meeting mine. "Let me make one thing clear. Rob Thompson is an idiot, and there's no chance I'd let him touch this case with a ten-foot pole."

I tilt my head, a frown tugging at my lips. "Then why would you assign him to it in the first place?"

"It was the only way to get you to cooperate," he states with a shrug. "You're far more stubborn than I gave you credit for."

A small smile tugs at my lips. "Why, thank you."

"It wasn't a compliment," he says with a straight face.

If I had any sense of self-preservation, I'd stop provoking him. Better yet, I'd leave and never visit the fourth floor. But clearly, I've thrown caution to the wind since I'm still here, staring at the man who can make or break my career.

"This case will require long nights, extensive research, and careful coordination with my client and the team. This project demands the best, and the glowing recommendations from your past employer suggest that includes you."

"Dawson, I'm flattered, truly, but—"

He holds out his hand to silence me. "What's the real reason you refuse to work with me? Is it because of what happened between us at Steel & Ink?" he asks, lowering his voice.

Yes.

"No, that has nothing to do with it," I lie, dropping my gaze. "I've only been here a week. I'm sure one of the more seasoned paralegals would be happy to assist you."

Dawson doesn't say a word as he gets out of his chair and comes to perch on the edge of his desk. His jaw is tight and his eyes are narrowed, leaving me unsure if he's angry or in deep concentration. My breath hitches when his leg brushes against mine, and the brief touch sends a tremor through me.

He shifts closer, taking a deep breath. "You smell like pineapple and coconut," he murmurs.

My knuckles turn white as I grip my armrest. "It's my shampoo," I whisper.

"I like it… a lot."

I force myself to remain still, my body coming alive with him so close. My pulse is pounding in my ears as he traces my jawline with his thumb. Though it seems like an innocent gesture, the undercurrent of desire in his lingering touch sends my heart racing.

His shirt sleeve has risen, giving me a glimpse of a rose tattoo. I'm mesmerized by the intricate design, at how the bold ink is in stark contrast to his skin. My hand inches closer, itching to trace the lines. I pause when I notice Dawson, his intense gaze locked on mine. His eyes have a glimmer of fascination, and it could be my imagination, but I swear he leans in a fraction, almost inviting my touch.

The sound of approaching footsteps causes him to withdraw. He remains perched on his desk, pretending to adjust his tie as if he'd been preparing to have a serious conversation, not on the verge of being caught in a compromising situation with one of his employees.

Dawson's dangerous—not just because of his reputation, but because if I let him, he'll find a way to chip at my defenses, making it impossible to resist his charm. And I can't afford to let my guard down when my future is on the line.

No matter how enticing he might be.

Jeremy, the head investigative specialist at Thompson & Tate, knocks on the doorframe. "Is now a bad time?" he asks, eyeing Dawson, who's scowling at him.

"What do you need?" Dawson snaps.

"I have the reports you asked for, sir." Jeremy holds a folder but doesn't move from his spot on the threshold.

Dawson exhales sharply. "Let me see." He drums his fingers against the desk, his impatience evident.

Poor Jeremy visibly trembles as he rushes to pass Dawson the folder before scurrying out of the room. Dawson flips through the documents and I seize the chance to slip out of my chair, ready to make a beeline for the door. But before I can take more than a step, his hand gently grabs my wrist.

"Hang on. We're not finished." His tone is firm but calm.

"I'd like to get back to work if that's okay with you." I fold my arms across my chest, waiting for him to make the next move.

His eyes dart to my mouth before meeting my eyes. "Go on." He nods toward the door. "But my decision stands. I'll email your new schedule this afternoon."

I sigh, not wanting to push him past his limit.

I'm halfway across the room when Dawson calls out after me. "Oh, and Reese?"

I turn back to face him. "Yeah?"

"If Rob gives you any trouble with your new schedule, let me know and I'll take care of it."

My eyebrows arch in disbelief. Given the way he treats everyone else, it's hard to reconcile him letting his guard down to show warmth and kindness, especially to someone in my position. And I'm intrigued by the prospect of uncovering that side of him, the one he hides behind his brusque exterior.

"Thank you, Mr. Tate."

I'm already bracing for Rob's sour mood when he sees my new schedule as I make my way downstairs. It's only my second week here, and I'm now required to spend more time with the man I've been fantasizing about for the past three months.

How much more complicated can it get?

CHAPTER 5

Dawson

It's Friday, and I've been cooped up in my office for hours reviewing a contract when my phone pings on my desk.

> **Mickey:** One of your customers called and wants to book a tattoo appointment for tomorrow night.

> **Dawson:** That's fine. I'll fit them in.

> **Mickey:** You coming into the shop tonight?

> **Dawson:** Yeah. I have a cover-up session.

> **Mickey:** See you then.

Mickey gave me my first tattoo—the compass. I got it the week before I started college. It was a symbol of my journey to forge a new path and a reminder that I'm in control of my own destiny. After that I was hooked, and he's been responsible for all my ink since. He used to talk about wanting to own his own shop someday, but said he could never afford it.

A few years later, I had a meeting with a client at their office down the street and stumbled on Steel & Ink while walking past.

It used to be a dry cleaner that went out of business, and the layout looked like it would be perfect for a tattoo parlor. I brought up my idea of converting the place to Mickey, offering him a stake in the business and the freedom to run it however he wanted. My only condition being that I had my own station. He's the only one at the shop who knows about my day job, but we rarely talk about it.

When my phone buzzes again I check to see it's a message from Harrison Stafford.

> **Harrison:** You down for getting a drink at the bar tonight?
>
> **Dawson:** Sure.
>
> **Harrison:** Meet at 11?
>
> **Dawson:** Sounds good. You're buying.
>
> **Harrison:** I always pay.
>
> **Dawson:** Fine by me.

The bar is just down the street from the tattoo parlor, so I should have plenty of time to finish my appointment before we meet up.

Harrison and I met a few years ago when he needed help with a disgruntled client. Despite being handed the keys to his family's business, he works his ass off. Since taking the reins as CEO of Stafford Holdings, it has become the most lucrative real estate firm in the country. He's earned a reputation for his no-nonsense attitude and uncompromising approach to business, which I appreciate.

He travels more often than not, but we occasionally meet up at a local dive bar for a drink when we're both free.

I'm about to put my phone away and check my email when it rings, and a rare smile crosses my lips when I see who it is.

"Hi, Martha."

"Don't *hi Martha* me," she scolds. "You have some explaining to do. Colby and I haven't heard from you in over a week, and we've been worried sick."

"Correction. Martha has been anxious. I figured you were just too busy running the firm and playing hardball with opposing counsel to call," Colby interjects with a chuckle. "If you were a public defender like me, you'd be making a difference instead of raking in millions with no time for yourself."

"Don't pay him any mind, honey," Martha says. "We're so proud of you, isn't that right, Colby?" I can only imagine Martha staring him down, silently daring him to disagree with her.

"At least one of you misses me," I quip.

Colby likes to hassle me about my career choice, but he's been my biggest supporter since day one. Martha and Colby Tate may not be related to me by blood, but they're my parents in all the ways it matters.

I was placed in foster care when I was four years old. My birth mom was an addict and couldn't handle the responsibility of taking care of me. Without any information on my birth dad and no family to speak of, she handed me over to Child Protective Services.

Due to my frequent tantrums and emotional outbursts, I wasn't adopted. As a result, I was passed from one foster home to the next.

By the time I was fifteen, I'd had several run-ins with the cops and accepted the harsh reality that if nothing changed, my life would be defined by crime and poverty. However, I caught a break when Colby was assigned as my public defender, and in many ways, the Tates saved my life.

He persuaded the judge handling my case to give me one last chance, since the charges weren't violent or drug related. I remember his advice like it was yesterday. *You hold the power to change your future, son. Use this opportunity to make better decisions and do what it takes to become a version of yourself that you can be proud of.*

His words of wisdom led me to change my mindset, and I promised myself that I would do everything in my power to make sure that I never went back.

Two decades later, I've nearly achieved it all: a luxurious house with a rooftop pool, a successful career, and enough money in the bank to fund a small country. Yet, the irrational fear of returning to poverty and drifting through life unnoticed still haunts me.

"Are you all right, Dawson," Martha asks, snapping me out of my thoughts. "You sound exhausted. Do you need me to have anything delivered?"

"I'm fine. It's just been a busy week at the office." I get up from my desk to stand at the window that overlooks the bustling city streets below. "What are you both doing at home during the day anyway? Should I be worried?"

On Wednesdays, Colby usually represents his clients in court, while Martha runs her interior design agency out of their home in New Haven, Connecticut. When I was accepted into law school at Yale, Colby accepted a job offer in the area. After I graduated and moved back to New York, they chose to stay in New Haven because they loved their house and the peace and quiet their neighborhood provided compared to the hustle and bustle of the city.

"Today is the anniversary of the day we met, so I'm taking Martha out for a little adventure to revisit some of our favorite memories."

I rub my hand across my neck. "That's right. Happy anniversary," I offer.

After everything they've been through, they deserve to celebrate every milestone, regardless of how small.

"Thanks, honey," Martha says, her voice full of warmth.

Before I came into their lives, they had separated and were considering divorce. They struggled with infertility for years and were eventually told they couldn't have kids. After reconciling, they applied to become licensed foster parents. They were approved just days before my case was resolved and agreed to take me in. Although it's unusual for foster kids to stay with their lawyers, CPS made an exception for my case, and Martha and Colby adopted me a year later.

I shake off my wandering thoughts. "Well, I'll let you get back to your date," I tell them, not wanting to hold them up any longer. "Thanks for checking in on me."

"We're always here for you, son," Colby says.

"Always," Martha adds, and I can hear the smile in her voice. "Have a great rest of your day, honey."

"You too, talk later," I say before hanging up.

Every day, I'm reminded of how grateful I am for the love, sacrifice, and support that Martha and Colby bring into my life. I will never take their generosity for granted.

I slide my hand into my pants pocket and look back down at the street to find it's even busier than before. Lunch hour is wrapping up, so everyone is rushing back to their offices. I catch a glimpse of red hair among the moving figures below. Even from four stories up, I can make out the emerald-green scarf Reese was wearing when she brought me a file earlier this morning.

When I assigned her to report to both me and Rob, I assumed she'd spend half her time on my floor. Instead, she's spent this past week at her desk downstairs, and our interactions are mostly through emails and texts.

I don't normally share my personal number with employees, but for her, I didn't hesitate.

There's something about her presence that makes me want to keep her close. It's an irrational thought, but that doesn't stop me from contemplating how to remedy the situation.

One way or another, I'm going to find a way to see her more often.

It's relatively quiet when I arrive at the bar. There are several empty tables and only a couple of patrons playing pool and darts. The bartender gives me a nod as I pass, signaling that he'll bring my usual two fingers of brandy over shortly.

Harrison is settled at the far end of the bar, his Old Fashioned untouched, while he taps away on his phone. He glances up when I slide into the empty stool next to him.

"Took you long enough." His muscular arms fill out the sleeves of his short-sleeve polo as he lifts his drink to his mouth.

"Something came up that I had to deal with," I mutter.

"And they call *me* a workaholic," he says.

Harrison assumes I spend my weekends like he does—building my ever-growing empire. He has no idea about Steel & Ink or the sleeves of tattoos concealed beneath my dress shirt.

I'm a product of my past.

Becoming a lawyer was a practical decision. A means to an end to secure a stable financial future. While owning a tattoo parlor is personal, it's my way to connect with people who use ink to share their stories and express themselves. Tattooing provides me with a necessary escape from both the formal confines of my legal career and the memory of my checkered past.

The bartender brings my drink over. "Thanks," I say, swirling it before taking a generous sip and savoring the burn. "How's business?" I ask Harrison.

"Busy. Cash and Everly are back in London, and I've been working closely with them and the European division to oversee the Townstead International acquisition. Meanwhile, Stafford Holdings is booming. It's been a challenge managing it all." He runs his hands through his black hair that's styled in a tapered fade. "How are things at the firm?"

"I finally convinced Wes Irving that he should hire me as his lawyer," I say with a smug smile.

He's been wrapped in litigation with his ex-business partner for four years. I'm confident that I can resolve this before Christmas with the right leverage.

"Damn, that's impressive, congrats," Harrison says, barely glancing up from his phone, his attention focused on whatever is on the screen.

"Thanks." I throw back the rest of my drink, motioning for the bartender to bring me another. "Are you texting a woman?" I taunt, noting the pointed glare Harrison shoots me. "Oh, that's right, you don't have time for anything but work these days," I say with an amused chuckle.

"Says the guy who treats his office like his second home and only has casual flings."

He has a point. The only women I sleep with agree to my terms—casual sex with no expectations of a long-term relationship, and I never spend the night. Some encounters have been one-night stands, while others have lasted a few days. Unfortunately for me, only one woman has been on my mind during the past four months, and it's someone off-limits.

The problem is, I've never been this intrigued by a woman before, especially not after one kiss. I can't seem to control how often Reese crosses my mind and it's maddening.

"Better watch your attitude, Harrison, or I'll make sure I cash in one of my favors when it's the most inconvenient for you."

"I don't doubt it," he mumbles sarcastically as he finishes off his drink.

The Stafford brothers ran into some legal trouble when acquiring Townstead International and came to me for advice. After my team did some digging, we discovered that the former owner, Richard, had all but driven his business into the ground with embezzlement, tax evasion, kickbacks—the list goes on.

As a lawyer who doesn't shy away from controversy or difficult situations, I agreed to help Harrison deal with Richard with the caveat that aside from my exorbitant retainer, he and his brothers owed me a couple of favors. Besides, I'd never miss out on the chance to make a grown man quake in his boots or watch him sign away his livelihood when he's been a symbol of corruption, putting his family at risk in the process. "Now that your brothers have settled down, does that mean you're next?"

Harrison shakes his head. "Not a chance. They got lucky finding incredible partners, but my priority is business. There's no one who could handle a man who spends twenty hours a day running a multibillion-dollar company and is hardly ever home."

"Never say never." I smirk and lean back in my chair. "I'm sure there's someone out there who'd tolerate your grumpy ass and is willing to work around your busy schedule if they cared about you enough."

He glances across the room like he's lost in thought. "There's only one woman who fits that description, and she's the bane of my existence," he mutters.

"Damn, Harrison. You're in a dark mood tonight."

"And you're unusually upbeat," he counters. "You're normally the one in a foul mood. What gives?"

I run a hand over my mouth and consider what he said. Now that he mentions it, I'm in a notably good mood tonight when normally I'm rather irritable by the end of the week. It could have something to do with finding a way to see Reese more often at work. Even though it might take a few weeks to arrange, it has me feeling oddly optimistic.

"Guess I woke up on the right side of the bed today," I say to Harrison, shrugging it off. "Don't get used to it."

"Before I forget, here are those hockey tickets you asked for." He slides me an envelope. "Just so you know, it was a pain in the ass to get club seat season passes. They're as popular as a VIP pass for a sold-out Sovereign Kings concert. You're lucky I'm a part-owner." He played a year of professional hockey in his early twenties and still practices with the Mavericks to this day.

"Thanks, man. Send me the invoice for the tickets, and I'll send over the payment," I say, tucking the envelope into my suit pocket.

"You can count on it," Harrison says.

Besides asking about the occasional hookup, Harrison and I don't talk about personal matters, but I make it my job to know everything about my clients—he's no exception. While he's the closest thing I have to a friend, it's hard for me to let my guard down.

Growing up in foster care taught me that trust is a rare commodity. When I was thirteen, my best friend, Max, stole a pair of high-end sneakers. The police showed up at our foster home the next day and found the shoes hidden under my bed. The asshole framed me, and I was sent to juvie. Trying to explain my innocence would have been futile—foster kids are often unfairly judged because of their less-than-ideal circumstances.

That was my first of a string of run-ins with the police and time spent in juvenile detention. It's one of the reasons I avoid making friends or committing to serious relationships. Aside from Martha and Colby, I'm the only person I can rely on.

Along with the false robbery accusations, I was repeatedly arrested for vandalism while painting murals on public buildings and construction sites.

After moving in with the Tates, Martha gifted me a set of sketchpads and pencils. However, when she caught me trying to sneak out of the house with a backpack of spray paints, she and Colby turned the garage into a studio fit with several large canvases and paints, offering a creative outlet that wouldn't get me into more trouble. This sparked my love for storytelling through art, and the day I got my first tattoo, I knew I'd found my true passion.

Relaxing in my chair, I fold my arms. "Just so we're clear, the tickets don't count as one of my favors since you agreed to get the tickets before you owed me," I say with a smug expression.

"Figured you'd say that," Harrison complains. "What the hell do you need two favors for anyway?"

From my observation, favors are reserved for close friends and family. Since I refuse to ever be in someone's debt, I prefer collecting favors when people owe me to avoid any misconceptions about obligations. In my opinion, it's better to keep things clear and straightforward.

I shrug. "Might as well have a couple in the bank for emergencies. Never know when I might need help hiding a dead body," I deadpan.

"You better not get me or my brothers into any legal trouble," Harrison warns.

I give him a pat on the back. "Lucky for you, you've got a great lawyer."

His alarmed expression only makes me chuckle. Cashing in these favors might turn out to be entertaining after all.

CHAPTER 6

Dawson

THE NEXT AFTERNOON, I PULL UP TO THE APARTMENT building Christian and his mom live in to find him waiting outside on the curb.

He's sporting the baseball cap I got him at a Yankees game last year that keeps his shaggy blond hair from falling in his eyes. He has an athletic build with broad shoulders from playing football and baseball.

I cover the cost for him to explore any extracurricular activities he's interested in, wanting him to have every opportunity I never had growing up.

"Hey, Dawson," he says, grinning.

I hop off my bike and give him a fist bump. "Hey, kid."

"When are you going to give me a ride?" He adjusts his baseball cap as he admires my limited-edition Confederate FA-13 Combat Bomber. "I'd be the coolest kid at school if you dropped me off on this thing."

He's only fourteen, but in many ways he's more focused and disciplined than most adults. With his mom working long hours as a nurse at the local hospital, Christian helps with the household chores and cooks so she has a meal waiting for her after a long shift.

"Sorry, Christian. I promised your mom I wouldn't take you on my bike."

He shrugs. "Yeah, well, I'm still going to keep asking." He runs his hand over the bike. "One of these days she'll come around."

I've got to give him credit for his perseverance.

I pull out an envelope from my leather jacket and hand it to him. "In my opinion, this is even better than going for a ride."

Christian gives me a skeptical look when he opens it up, his eyes growing wide when he takes out the booklet of tickets. "Are you serious? Is this what I think it is?" He's grinning from ear to ear.

A swell of pride fills me as I see his face light up. After everything he's been through, witnessing the joy in his eyes means everything. I'll always go the extra mile for this kid, no matter what.

"If you guessed season tickets to the Mavericks, you would be right," I say.

"This is incredible. Thanks, Dawson—you're the best big brother ever," Christian exclaims, throwing his arms around me in a hug.

I pause briefly before wrapping one arm around him in a side hug. Growing up in foster care, most of the physical touches I received were harsh and impersonal, aside from the occasional handshake or hug from a case worker, and even those were few and far between.

Christian and I might not be part of a Big Brothers Big Sisters program, but it became a running joke when we started hanging out. Before long, he was calling me his big brother and I've found that I don't mind it.

I tousle his hair. "Sure thing, kid."

"Can I go show Koda? He's our new neighbor and loves the Mavericks too."

"Yeah, I'll wait out here. You still down to get tacos and ice cream?"

"Hell yeah." He grins. "My mom's shift ends in an hour. Can we get her something, too? She loves tacos."

"Of course, but watch your language," I warn.

He crosses his arms, a stern expression on his face. "How come? You swear all the time."

"I'm allowed to because I'm an adult. Plus, if your mom thinks I'm being a bad influence, she won't let us hang out anymore."

"Fine," he mumbles." But someday, I'll be an adult, and then you can't tell me what to do."

I chuckle. "We'll see about that. Now go show Koda your tickets so we can go. I'm starving."

As he runs off, I can't help thinking about how far he's come since we met.

Two years ago, Colby called and asked if I could help one of his former colleagues at the New York City Public Defender's Office with Christian's juvenile case.

Christian had been caught shoplifting a pair of earrings from a high-end boutique on the Upper East Side, and the store owner was insistent on pressing charges. He told the police that his mom was working three jobs to make ends meet, and he just wanted to get her something nice for her birthday.

Generally, petty theft doesn't warrant a stint in juvenile detention. But the judge handling Christian's case was the same one I had when I was falsely accused of stealing shoes and wanted to make an example of Christian.

I agreed to help with the case pro bono, unwilling to stand by and let him be unfairly punished by the same man who nearly ruined my life. After some digging, my team uncovered that this judge owns a stake in the juvenile detention center where he sends most offenders. The more kids he sends there, the greater his financial kickbacks.

Armed with a dossier brimming with blackmail, I paid the judge a visit. He publicly announced his retirement the next morning. Within a month, his life fell apart—his reputation was tarnished by a high-profile investigation, his bank account in the Cayman Islands was drained, and his luxury vacation home in Malibu was seized to pay his legal fees.

What can I say? When someone crosses me or those I care about, they suffer the consequences.

After Christian's case was dismissed, I asked his mom for permission to spend time with him. What started as monthly meetups evolved into a weekly routine. We usually grab a bite to eat and attend sporting events, and I go to his games when I can. I'm determined to make sure Christian has the chance to pursue his passions and build a future he's proud of, like Colby and Martha did for me.

My phone pings in my pocket, and I check to find I have a message from the firm's team chat system. I'd sent Reese a message earlier requesting her review of the discovery documents from the opposing counsel on the Irving case and that she create an index for easy reference.

I wasn't expecting a response from her until Monday, but I can't deny the boost my mood gets at seeing her reply.

> **Reese:** I just saw your email. I'm not at home today, or I'd get to it sooner.
>
> **Dawson:** Did you read the whole email?
>
> **Reese:** Yes.
>
> **Dawson:** Then you saw my note about handling it on Monday?
>
> **Reese:** I did.
>
> **Dawson:** So, you're messaging me over the weekend because you miss me? I'm touched.

Reese: Don't flatter yourself.

Reese: Rob expects me to reply to emails over the weekend, so I assumed you'd want the same.

A growl rumbles from my throat. Rob has a habit of taking advantage of employees, and if I find out he's been mistreating Reese, he's finished. Fuck my promise to Maxwell to keep him on at the firm.

I run my fingers through my hair, frustrated with my line of thinking. There's no rational explanation for why Reese has this kind of effect on me. She's just a paralegal who happens to work for me, or at least that's the story I'm sticking to.

Dawson: You're officially banned from working on the weekends.

Reese: What if I like breaking the rules?

Dawson: If I didn't know better, I'd think you were trying to rile me up, Ms. Taylor.

Reese: Now why would I want to do that, Mr. Tate?

I groan at her use of my last name, recalling how it sounds when she says it in person. Damn, this woman is fun to spar with, and the best part is, she gives as good as she gets.

While most people cower in my presence, she boldly puts me in my place. Toeing the line between playful banter and stepping over it is a dangerous yet exhilarating game.

Dawson: Of course you are, Ms. Taylor. Forgive me.

Reese: See you on Monday.

Dawson: Looking forward to it, Red.

As I tuck my phone back into my pocket, I realize that for the first time in ages I'm looking forward to going into the office on Monday.

CHAPTER 7

Reese

TWO WEEKS LATER

THE PAST TWO WEEKS HAVE BEEN AN ADJUSTMENT AT work, with me having to learn to balance reporting to both Rob and Dawson.

They are complete opposites. Rob is rude and demeaning, always assigning me pointless tasks and calling them urgent. Whereas Dawson values my time and gives me meaningful work that challenges me. And unlike Rob, he hasn't raised his voice at me once.

I can't deny that I enjoy our daily exchanges and verbal duels. Even on the longest days, I look forward to our interactions— strictly in a professional capacity, of course.

If only that were true.

Dawson occupies my thoughts more often than I care to admit. Whenever we're in the same room, my gaze drifts to him as if he's the sun and I'm caught in his gravitational pull, unable to break free. I wonder if he feels the same magnetic draw toward me or if it's all in my head.

This is why working together was a bad idea.

The fact that my desk is on a different floor is my one reprieve, keeping our encounters somewhat limited.

This past weekend away from the office also served as a nice distraction, even though it passed in a blur. I had to cancel my Saturday study session with Noah when a pipe burst in my kitchen. Unfortunately, it had to be replaced, and I was forced to call an emergency plumber that put me out eight hundred dollars. On the bright side, I was able to visit Grams and join her at Oak Ridge's weekly bingo night.

The ding of the elevator brings me back to the present.

On my way to the office this morning, I had to stop by a bakery on the other side of town to get Rob's breakfast.

I stop short when I notice Stacey, a receptionist from another department, sitting at my desk, typing on her laptop. All my things are missing, and my mind is racing as I glance around to make sure I'm in the right place.

Rob was angry when Dawson had me spend yesterday afternoon on research for the Irving case instead of helping him sort through stacks of outdated legal briefs and preparing document summaries. I wouldn't put it past him to have me fired, but the pressing question is whether he's actually succeeded in doing so.

I'm doing my best to refrain from panicking when Rob storms out of his office. Steam is practically coming out of his ears as he snatches his cappuccino and jelly-filled donut from my hand. I wince when a splash of coffee burns my finger.

"You're late," he barks.

I frown, glancing at the clock. I'm ten minutes early, but it's no use arguing with him when he's in one of his moods.

"Can you tell me why Stacey is at my desk?" I ask, broaching the subject tentatively.

He fixes me with a glare over his cup while slurping his coffee.

"Because I don't have time to make the trip upstairs whenever I need something from you," he sneers.

I furrow my brow. "I'm sorry, I don't understand."

He exhales sharply. "Dawson informed me this morning that you're moving to his floor. Apparently, he can't be bothered to track you down whenever he needs something but expects me to," he whines. "Don't for a moment think you're off the hook. You're still my paralegal, is that clear?"

"Crystal," I deadpan.

Confrontation is something I usually like to avoid when the outcome could lead to unnecessary conflict. It's why I've seldom pushed back against Rob—it's not worth the hassle. But today, I'm feeling especially daring and give him a piece of my mind.

"Your attitude is unacceptable. If you think—"

"Reese, there you are." Dawson cuts Rob off as he strides down the hall toward us.

Rob scowls, clearly irritated by the interruption.

A group of first-year associates scramble to clear a path for Dawson, and everyone at their desks avoids looking at him. It's obvious that apart from me, everyone in the office is petrified of him and doesn't dare to get in his way. Even Rob's bravado visibly wanes as he shrinks back when Dawson approaches. It serves him right for throwing his weight around and acting like he's in charge.

Dawson gives Rob a pointed glare. "Why are you loitering in the hallway? Don't you have work to do?"

"Rob was just telling me I have a new desk assignment," I interject.

"*Someone* has been monopolizing your time and forgets I'm the lead counsel on the Irving case. I need you close by to help keep it running smoothly," Dawson says, casting a disapproving glance at Rob, who remains silent like the coward he is. He has no qualms about talking badly about Dawson behind his back, but when push comes to shove, he folds like a cheap suit. It's almost laughable. "Come, Reese, I need you upstairs," Dawson adds, turning on his heel toward the elevator.

I drag my hand across my face, exasperated. How could he interfere… again? It's not like I enjoy working with Rob, but Dawson keeps steamrolling my choices. I wish he could see that my input matters. This is my job, and I'd rather not be caught in his constant tug-of-war with Rob.

"Are you coming?" Dawson calls over his shoulder.

I adjust my purse on my shoulder as I rush to catch up, finding it challenging to do so in heels.

When we reach the elevator, he gestures for me to enter first, placing a hand on my lower back as he ushers me inside. My traitorous heart races, and heat spreads across my cheeks.

Any other person would reprimand him for infringing on professional decorum, yet my body responds to his touch like a moth to a flame. My logical side reminds me that the man touching me is my boss—my *off-limits* boss.

As much as I try to push it aside, my mind replays our kiss at the tattoo parlor like it has thousands of times before.

Dawson's hands band around my waist as he tugs me close to his chest. He kisses along my jawline, flicking his tongue along the seam of my lips, coaxing me to let him in, and the warmth of his mouth… It's incredible. The way he growls makes my pulse quicken, a dangerous thrill running through me.

I revel in the way my legs feel wrapped around his body, his strong hands holding me in place, like a promise not to let me go. God, the way his cock feels rubbing against my core, and my nipples grow achy, desperate for his touch.

I'm jolted back to the present when the elevator doors close. When I notice that Dawson and I are alone, I take a deep breath and ask, "Why did you move me to your floor?"

He turns toward me, his eyes meeting mine. "Like I told Rob, I want you there so you're close when I need you."

A shiver ripples through me. He only means in a professional capacity, but there's something in his voice that I can't quite place—a mix of authority and unspoken desire. Which shouldn't send heat rushing to my cheeks, but I feel the warmth spreading regardless. Being around him always leaves me feeling both unsteady and exhilarated, and I look away, hoping he doesn't notice my reaction.

I smooth down the crease in my skirt and say, "It would have been nice to know about being reassigned to a different floor, that's all."

Dawson lets out a sigh. "Why does it feel like you're unhappy about something I've done every time we're alone?"

I tilt my head to face him, finding the courage to speak my mind. "Must be your talent for getting under my skin."

He reaches out to gently place his hand on my arm. "I'm only trying to help you."

I scoff. "Help me? What you're doing is causing me more problems."

His brow furrows. "How so?"

His interference not only aggravates Rob, but I'm worried it could lead others to question the nature of our relationship since I'm new and already getting preferential treatment. Especially given that Dawson never escorts anyone to his office unless they're about to be terminated or face serious disciplinary action.

"My god, you're infuriating, Red," he mutters when I don't answer. "Most paralegals would jump at the chance to work with a managing partner, yet here you are, trying to escape me every chance you get."

I blink rapidly and pull back, moving my head to look at him. "Lucky? Do you realize how it looks for a new hire to receive special treatment?" I inquire with a humorless laugh. "The last thing I want is to risk my reputation by being shown favoritism from the boss."

"What if that's exactly what's going on?" His tone is sincere. My breath catches. "Explain."

He hesitates, his gaze lingering on my mouth for a long moment. "I like being around you, Ms. Taylor, and if you haven't noticed, I can't stand most people," he says with a half-hearted chuckle. "Frankly, I don't give a damn what other people think, and if there's someone that I trust and enjoy spending time with, I'm going to have them report directly to me. It's that simple."

My mouth falls open in disbelief that Dawson Tate, of all people, just admitted that he likes having me around.

I should probably be upset that he openly admitted I'm being treated differently. From a professional standpoint, it's inappropriate. Yet, it's impossible to shake the butterflies that take flight in my stomach when I hear that he might care more than he should.

Seeing a glimpse of his unguarded side makes me want to share something in return.

I let out a long breath and glance over at him. "When I found Stacey at my desk this morning, I thought I might have been fired." My voice comes out in a whisper.

"Shit, I'm sorry," Dawson says, pausing to run a hand through his hair. "That wasn't my intention. I was worried if I told you ahead of time, you would have said no," he admits.

"And what if I had?"

He closes the gap between us. "I would have kept trying until you said yes."

I place my hand on his chest, my fingers linger on the top button of his dress shirt—torn between pushing him away and pulling him closer to get a better look.

With his striking blue eyes, tailored suits, and air of authority, he's the epitome of sex appeal, and I wish he didn't have such a profound effect on me.

Like he can read my mind, he shifts forward, his nose grazing mine, the air between us humming with electricity.

"I'm trying to be good, Ms. Taylor," Dawson murmurs, his breath hot against my mouth, daring me to close the last sliver of space between us. My fingers curl into his collar and every fiber of my being tenses in anticipation, caught between a mix of excitement and trepidation.

Just when I think he might bring his mouth to mine, he reaches over to press the button for the top floor. "I almost forgot. Can't imagine why," he murmurs, an uncharacteristic smirk playing on his lips as the elevator begins its ascent.

I take a step back, visibly shaken.

That was a close call… too close.

I've got to get my hormones in check, or I'm going to be in serious trouble. There would have been no plausible explanation if someone had found me pressed against my boss with my hand on his collar.

I run my hand through my hair, doing my best to compose myself before we reach our floor. When the elevator chimes, the doors slide open, and Dawson holds out his hand. "After you."

"Thank you."

On my way to his office, I pause when I notice the desk and chair set up just outside. My belongings, including my laptop and monitor, are neatly arranged on top, accompanied by a glass vase of sunflowers, baby's breath, and eucalyptus.

I gently touch a sunflower petal as I inhale the fresh scent. "The flowers are lovely."

They remind me of the bouquets my grandpa used to bring home every Friday for me and Grams. He knew how much I loved them—I was constantly doodling flowers in my notebook and on my sneakers. Even when money was tight, he always made sure he brought an arrangement home for us both.

"I'm glad you like them," Dawson says, the ghost of a smile on his lips. "Why don't you try the chair."

As soon as I sink into the cushion, I groan. "This is amazing. Who would have thought a chair could be this comfortable."

"Last week, I passed your desk on the way to a meeting and saw that you were shifting uncomfortably in your other chair. I wanted to make sure you had something more comfortable. This one is ergonomic and custom-designed."

I stare up at him, speechless.

He noticed?

On my first day, I had a decent office chair, but when Rob saw it, he insisted we swap. His chair was old and had little cushioning left. He could have asked for a new one but chose to inconvenience me rather than deal with the replacement process.

Dawson's unexpected kindness is touching, and I shouldn't read into it, but it's hard not to. It's another example of him going out of his way for me when he doesn't extend the same effort to everyone else.

He is such a contradiction—a man who commands authority and berates those who fall short. Yet he orders me a custom chair and buys me flowers to make me feel more at home in my new space...

Dawson clears his throat, breaking the silence. "I have a call with a client. You should get back to work. I'll let you know when I need you." He strides past me, shutting his office door behind him.

Okay then.

A notification from our team chat system pops up on my laptop—it's a message from Grace, the paralegal I met at the all-hands meeting during my first week. We chat occasionally during those rare lulls in between projects.

> **Grace:** Glad we're on the same floor now. It's nice to have a friendly face around!
>
> **Reese:** Thank you! Happy to be here.

Although I'm relieved to be away from Rob, my encounter

with Dawson in the elevator proves that being near him every day isn't a good idea. We're strictly co-workers who kissed once and now almost a second time, but I'm determined not to blur the lines between our personal and professional lives further. Now, if only I could stop thinking about what might have happened if we had more time alone in the elevator.

> **Grace:** When I went by your desk earlier, I saw the bouquet. They're stunning.

> **Reese:** Right? I think they add a nice touch to the space.

> **Grace:** They are! Whoever sent them was very thoughtful.

> **Reese:** Yes, they are.

I keep my response vague. I'm not about to tell her that Dawson bought me flowers.

> **Grace:** I'm glad you're not working for Rob full-time anymore. You deserve better.

> **Grace:** But don't let Dawson push you around either, okay?

> **Reese:** I won't.

> **Grace:** I've got to run to a meeting, but let's have lunch soon?

> **Reese:** Looking forward to it.

Hopefully I can find the time. Between Rob and Dawson, my workload has significantly increased, and I have a feeling things at the firm are only going to get busier. Now if I could just focus my attention back on work, and not the lingering scent of sandalwood and leather.

CHAPTER 8

Reese

MY STOMACH GROWLS LOUDLY AS I GLANCE AT THE clock, noting it's past nine thirty. The only thing I've had to eat today was a stale egg salad sandwich from the lobby vending machine that I scarfed down between projects.

Rob showed up right before lunch with fourteen boxes of documents, demanding they be filed by the end of the day. After I finished, Dawson asked me to join a conference call to take notes and help draft a contract.

I hoped to make it home at a decent time so I could squeeze in a study session for the LSAT, but I couldn't turn down substantive work. Dawson may be insufferable, but at least he assigns tasks related to my role, unlike Rob, who only has me running errands and filing paperwork.

Aside from Dawson and me, everyone on our floor else has gone home for the night. I'm tempted to order takeout even though it's not in my budget when the elevator doors open, and a young man heads in my direction with several large brown paper bags in tow.

"Can I help you?" I ask.

"I have a delivery for Dawson Tate." He holds up the bags in his hand. "Looks like someone's working late tonight."

"Yeah, it's been a busy day," I say.

His gaze shifts between Dawson's office and me, his expression playful. "If you ever want a change of scenery, I know a great place down the street—the best noodles in the city." He flashes me a grin. "It would be more fun than being stuck here all night, and it comes with good company."

"That does sound fun," I say with a polite smile. "But I'm usually working late, and I'm sure my boss would notice if I took an extended dinner break when we're in the middle of an important case."

"You're right, I would," Dawson interrupts as he exits his office. "If you want noodles, Reese, I'll have them delivered." The courier fidgets under Dawson's intense scrutiny, his eyes darting between me and Dawson, trying to gauge the situation.

"Sorry I'm late, sir," he manages to say. "They were short-staffed in the kitchen tonight, and I got here as fast as I could."

Dawson's expression remains impassive. "If you'd kept your attention on delivering my order instead of flirting with my paralegal, you might not have run behind schedule."

"Yes, sir," he replies, giving Dawson a wary look as he hands him the bags.

Could Dawson be jealous?

I cover my mouth with my hand to hide a smile at the silly notion. He's likely just irritated that he didn't get his food sooner.

The courier doesn't wait around, hurrying toward the exit. His steps are brisk, and he consciously avoids looking back. I don't blame him.

As the courier walks away, I notice Dawson's clenched jaw

as he stares in his direction. I place my hand on his arm to get his attention, and when he turns to look at me, his expression softens.

"Are you all right? You seem a little tense," I say with a hint of amusement.

Dawson's brows knit together, still scowling at the courier who's just stepping into the elevator. "He was a little too friendly with you, don't you think?"

I pull my hand away and prop my elbows on my desk, resting my chin against my hands. I'm rather enjoying watching Dawson get worked up over something so small.

One corner of my mouth lifts up into a subtle smile. "He was just being nice."

Dawson snorts. "Yeah, if nice is code for trying to score a date with a beautiful woman."

I stare at him wide-eyed, unsure if I heard him right. Did Dawson Tate just call me beautiful? Whether or not he meant it, I'm still as giddy as a schoolgirl. Despite my best efforts, butterflies beat wildly in my stomach. And I rather like the idea that he could be jealous, even if it's only a figment of my imagination.

"Well, regardless of his intentions, I would have declined his offer."

"Is that so?"

I sit up in my chair, tilting my chin to maintain eye contact. "Definitely. There's no chance I'm adding a boyfriend to the mix when I have you to deal with," I tease.

"Lucky for me, being the one who gets your undivided attention."

I chew on the inside of my lips, enjoying our playful banter far more than I should. My brain scrambles for a way to change the subject, and that's when I notice the bags in Dawson's hands.

"That looks like a lot of food. Are you having a late-night meeting with another department that I haven't heard about?"

Dawson shakes his head. "No. I figured you must be hungry

but wasn't sure what you liked, so I ordered one of everything from my favorite restaurant."

"You bought me food?"

"Of course. I asked you to stay late and I can't very well have you fainting on me now, can I?" He chuckles, his eyes crinkling in the corners.

I like seeing this relaxed side of him.

"No, we couldn't have that," I concede.

"Come on. Let's dig in before the food gets cold." He goes into his office, and I trail behind. "What's going to happen to the leftovers?" There are at least ten takeout boxes, and there's no way we'll eat a fraction of the food he ordered.

"Don't worry. The first-year associates on the third floor are pulling an all-nighter, so whatever we don't eat, you can take to them."

"That's very generous of you."

He takes out the boxes, and sets them on his desk for me to see.

"Have your pick." He waves to the food. "I'm not picky."

Each container is labeled, including options like wagyu beef sliders, grilled lamb chops, and lobster ravioli. It seems Dawson doesn't do anything halfway, even when it comes to take out.

I settle on the sliders served with fries and a side salad.

Dawson takes the lobster ravioli and once we're seated on the couch, I open my takeout container.

My stomach growls from the smell of grilled beef and toasted brioche. The sliders are perfectly browned, topped with caramelized onions and cheese, while the fries are crispy, and the side salad is drizzled with a vinaigrette.

"God, this all looks so good," I say, picking up my burger. "I haven't had a homemade meal in forever."

Dawson chuckles. "You're in the right profession if you

consider *this* homemade." He holds up a forkful of ravioli. "I practically live on takeout since I spend so much time at the office."

"What's your favorite food?" I ask. "Mine is shepherd's pie. But it has to have carrots and peas with homemade mashed potatoes on top. Add a sprinkle of cheese on top and it's the ultimate comfort food." *Grams used to make it for me every week.* "Although pumpkin spice lattes are a close favorite... " I trail off when I notice Dawson watching me.

I glance at him with uncertainty, worried my chatter is bothering him.

He scrunches his nose. "A latte is a drink, not a food," he points out.

"For some of us, it's practically a food group, Mr. Tate." I say teasingly.

He laughs softly, a warm glint dancing in his eyes.

It feels like a rare glimpse of his unfiltered side, making me wonder what else is hidden behind his normal guise.

I'm painfully aware of how close we're sitting, my nerves buzzing under my skin. Our intense chemistry crackles with an almost palpable energy. Even though it's just dinner, I sense a shift between us. Every time he does something thoughtful, another one of my defenses crumbles, leaving me to wonder how long I can hold out until my guard is down completely.

CHAPTER 9

Dawson

’M ON A CALL WITH THE OPPOSING COUNSEL FOR ONE OF MY cases the next morning. New information has come to light, making it necessary for us to discuss it privately before he shares the details with his client. However, so far, he hasn't grasped the severity of the situation.

"No, Donald, it's a shitty offer." I stare into the camera. "Let me be clear: if we're going to settle, you'll have to do much better than that. I know all about your client's extracurricular activities, and I've got the proof to back it up."

His face drains of color. "What the hell are you talking about? What evidence?"

"Did you actually believe my team wouldn't uncover your affair with your client? Seriously, Donald, how could you be that naive?" I pause to give my words a second to sink in. "I'm curious what your wife will say when she finds out. According to the infidelity clause in your prenup, Vickie stands to gain three vacation homes in both Florida and Bali if you're caught cheating. Should

I give her a call?" I lift my cell phone, the screen showing Vickie's number ready to dial.

"How the hell did you get a hold of my prenup?" Donald asks, visibly shaken.

I click my tongue in mock disappointment. "I'd expect someone of your caliber to recognize that information is power."

My team leaves no stone unturned when investigating opposing counsel and their clients. Even the smallest piece of information can tip the scales of a case. I rarely have to go to trial because our detailed groundwork typically leads to favorable settlements for my clients. But I make sure to be prepared for anything.

"Put your damn phone away," Donald demands through gritted teeth.

"What's in it for me and my client?" I ask, cutting to the chase.

It's best to take advantage when he's shell-shocked and unable to come up with a counter strategy.

"What do you want?" His voice trembles slightly.

I lean forward, my face devoid of emotion. "For starters, Viking International will sign over exclusive distribution rights to Jameson for the patented process. Plus, compensate him twenty million for their breach of contract."

"You can't be serious," Donald scoffs. "Exclusive rights were never on the table."

A sardonic grin plays on my face. "They are now," I state. "Unless you want Vickie and the media to find out that you've been fucking your biggest client for the last year. The choice is up to you."

"You're a real bastard; you know that, right?"

My finger hovers above the call button. "Do we have a deal or not?" Donald's eyes flare with indignation as he sweeps a pile of papers from his desk.

"If you're done with your tantrum, I have another call to make." I may be ruthless in negotiations, but I have no tolerance for those who play the system for selfish gain, especially at the expense of others. "What's it going to be, Donald?" I say in a clipped tone.

I keep my eyes trained on him through the computer screen as he silently runs through every possible escape route. The deepening frown on his face shows he's concluded that there's no way out. He either complies or suffers the consequences.

"Well?" I push when he doesn't respond.

He bites his lip so hard I'm surprised it doesn't bleed. "I'll draft the contract and send it to your office tomorrow once my client signs."

Being schooled by a lawyer half his age because of a string of reckless decisions must be a bitter pill to swallow. But I have no sympathy for him. He's made his bed; now he has to lie in it.

I tap my pen against my desk, narrowing my eyes. "You have until the end of the day."

"Fine," he growls. "But this means you won't call Vickie, right?"

"Correct. As long as you return the contract on time," I add, setting my phone down in good faith. "It was good doing business with you, Donald."

I end the call, not giving him a chance to counter. I predict I'll have the contract within the hour. He won't risk getting close to the deadline. Not with how much is at stake.

I'm deliberating over whether to pour myself a glass of whiskey now or wait until the signed contract is in my hands when I sense someone watching me.

I glance up to find Reese standing at the doorway, her eyes clouded with disappointment. "Why did you do that?" she whispers, her eyes widening when she realizes she spoke out loud.

"Do what?" I watch her closely as she tucks her hair behind her ear.

I brace myself for her disappointment. She must be upset that

I would resort to blackmail and use underhanded tactics. Reese tends to follow the rules, so I suspect my approach disappoints her. The idea of letting her down bothers me more than it should.

She gulps loudly. "Let Donald get away with cheating on his wife. Don't you think she has a right to know she's married to a fraud?" Reese steps forward, looking like she's unsure how I'll react.

My mouth falls open slightly, stunned. "Not everything is black and white, especially in this business," I say.

"No, but it's the right thing to do," she states with conviction. "Is money really worth allowing someone to get away with that kind of deception?"

God, she's adorable when she's all fired up.

I drum my fingers against my desk. "I might be aggressive and unyielding, but I won't back down when greedy adversaries try to exploit me or my clients."

She purses her lips. "Does opposing counsel do the same to you and your clients?"

I shake my head. "They wish they were so lucky. I do my research before working with a new client, and know exactly what I'm dealing with from the get-go to avoid any surprises."

Towing the line with Reese is the first impulsive thing I've done that could have repercussions for us both.

"For example, Harrison, one of my most reliable clients, is a billionaire who also happens to be the most straight-laced guy I know. I've found it's best not to judge a book by its cover." I use the same words she used on me the night at the tattoo shop. I leave out the part where I'm a billionaire, too, worried that will scare her off. "Why don't you have a look at those, and you'll see what I mean." I nod toward a pile of folders on my desk.

Reese takes a tentative step forward to retrieve them and sits on the couch in the corner. She flips through the documents, pausing at the dossier I compiled for Donald. I maintain one for opposing counsel and their clients, with detailed notes of potential leverage. It's important to have it ready, never knowing when the information might come in handy. Just like it did today.

She opens the dossier and begins reading the first page, a myriad of emotions flickering across her face, shifting from apprehension to confusion, and finally realization. After she's done, her shoulders slump as she nibbles on her lower lip.

With a downcast gaze, she whispers, "You were never going to let Donald off the hook."

I let a small grin slip. "No, Red, I wasn't."

A week after the funds are transferred from Donald's client, an encrypted email from an anonymous source will land in his wife's personal inbox, exposing all the evidence of Donald's affair. On top of that, all the illicit messages he sent to his client using his company's chat system will conveniently be brought to his business partners' attention by their IT department.

This will absolve me of any blame and guarantee that my client and I receive the compensation we're owed, along with the justice I'm after.

Reese shuts the folder, a quizzical look in her eyes. "Why didn't you tell me that in the first place?"

"Because it seems you want to paint me as a villain." I get up from my chair and take a seat next to her on the couch, allowing my leg to graze against hers. "Why is that?"

She's been working with me for two weeks and has been doing everything she can to create space between us—a stark contrast from the woman who bolted into my tattoo shop and kissed me with unguarded passion. And I want nothing more than to break down her walls and reignite the inferno we shared that night.

Admittedly, my desire goes beyond physical attraction. Since our conversation last night where she shared some of her favorite things, I find myself increasingly curious about her, and want to learn more about her interests and experiences. Every new thing she shares about herself is like a new tattoo on a sleeve—each one telling another part of her story.

Reese looks up, her green eyes meeting mine. "It's easier that way."

"What is?" I ask.

"If you were cold and cruel, I could pretend that I'm not attracted to you," she murmurs. "But instead, you're kind of decent under that gruff exterior. Even when you act like a jerk, it's clear you have good intentions."

I cup her chin, tilting her face to meet my gaze. I'm tempted to close the space between us and kiss her. She's the most alluring woman I've met, and I know that if I give in, I'll be consumed by an insatiable longing to do it again. Whether or not I'm ready to admit it, Reese Taylor could turn my world upside down if I let her.

But the reality is that she's my paralegal, and aside from our mutual chemistry, we don't seem to have much in common. While she's empathetic and understanding, always seeing the best in people, I'm suspicious and wary, quick to notice their flaws. I'm a guarded cynic masking my vulnerability with calculated indifference. I'm the guy who prefers a casual fling, and Reese strikes me as someone longing for commitment.

Like ink embedded in the skin, she's etched in my mind, impossible to erase. The space between us feels like a chasm I'm desperate to close, even though I shouldn't.

"You're so damn beautiful." I trace the freckles dotting the bridge of her nose with my thumb. "Being this close to you makes me want to throw out every rational notion and kiss you." Her eyes widen at my admission. "But I'm not going to do that."

She blinks up at me, her brow furrowed. "You're not?"

I force myself to remove my hand from her face. "No. Because I'm trying to be on my best behavior." *Even though I'd rather not have to be.* "Given how much this job means to you, I should never have put you in a position where it could be compromised."

Disappointment flickers across Reese's face, but she quickly replaces it with a polite smile. "I should get back to work."

She gets up, and I watch helplessly as she exits my office and closes the door behind her. My self-control is hanging by a thread, but somehow I refrain from going after her.

Over the next few hours, I pour myself into work reviewing a contract and taking a call with Jeremy, to review new information he's found for the Irving case. By the time I check my watch, I see that it's past noon. The rest of the office is at lunch, which means it's the one time I can walk the floor without interruption.

I'm relieved when I step into the hall and notice Reese's desk is empty. She must be out too. The last thing I need is the temptation of us being alone again today. She's addicting, and I'm powerless to her orbit, one that's drawn me in deeper with every fleeting glance and stolen moment. The more I try to steer clear, the harder it is to stay away.

An open book on her desk catches my eye. My curiosity is piqued when I take a closer look and discover it's an LSAT study guide, heavily annotated with highlights, margin notes, and sticky tabs marking various sections.

Reese hasn't mentioned that she was planning to go to law school. Normally I don't delve into my employees' personal lives. As long as they deliver results and meet my high expectations, I keep my distance. Yet, Reese has become the exception.

A pang of guilt hits me. I've been keeping her late almost every night, driven by my desire to have her close. I hadn't considered how it might affect her life outside of the office. With her demanding schedule, how does she manage to balance it all?

Since starting at Thompson & Tate, no matter how heavy her workload, she hasn't complained. I knew she was driven and committed to her job, but I didn't realize to what extent. Now that I have this small piece of information about her, it confirms my earlier sentiment—I want to know everything. It's a dangerous thought for someone who is supposed to be maintaining his distance.

While it's best that we keep things strictly professional, there's no harm in finding ways to ease her burden and make her workload more manageable.

Right?

CHAPTER 10

Reese

BEING THIS CLOSE TO YOU MAKES ME WANT TO THROW OUT *every rational notion and kiss you.*

Even a day later, Dawson's confession remains imprinted in my mind, and the memory of his touch still lingers. His hands were firm yet gentle as he cradled my face, and he looked at me, like nothing else in the world mattered.

If he had closed the last few inches between us, I would have kissed him. In that moment, all I wanted was to feel his mouth against mine.

Admittedly, my willpower is fading where he is concerned, and if we end up in a similar situation again, I don't think I'll be able to resist.

I force myself back to reality, fighting to keep my eyes open, I scan the email on my computer screen, struggling to make out the blurring text.

My supervisor at the club called me last night, begging me to cover for another server who was out sick. The club stayed open late, and after helping Noah with the closing duties and the long commute home, I didn't get to bed until four in the morning.

The one upside to working last night was the massive tip I got from being assigned to a bachelorette party on the second floor. It'll go toward my unexpected plumbing bill.

I pause, rubbing my eyes, ready for a break from trying to make sense of this email. I pull out my phone to check my messages.

> **Noah:** How are you feeling this morning?
>
> **Reese:** Like I've been hit by a freight train...
>
> **Noah:** On the bright side, at least you're not dealing with a hangover on top of your lack of sleep.
>
> **Reese:** True, but a hangover would mean I'd at least have some good stories to tell.
>
> **Reese:** How are you holding up?
>
> **Noah:** Thank god for the coffee shop around the corner from the courthouse.
>
> **Reese:** Coffee is always the answer.
>
> **Noah:** That might be the most brilliant thing you've ever said.
>
> **Reese:** I could totally go for a pumpkin spice latte.
>
> **Noah**: I'll get you one during our next study session.
>
> **Reese:** You're my hero.
>
> **Noah:** I always aim to please.

While I love the seasonal blend of cinnamon and nutmeg in a pumpkin spice latte, I usually save it for the homemade version due to the cost. However, I'm not one to refuse when Noah offers to buy me one.

I feel bad that we always study at his apartment and that I have an open invitation to spend the night whenever I want, yet he's never been to my house. If he found out that my furnace was out and that I didn't have hot water, he'd insist I move into his studio apartment until I could get it replaced. But I can't invade his space, especially since he likes to invite his dates over to spend the night. Noah's social life is thriving, despite him being just as busy as I am.

I place my phone back on my desk and move to review my work calendar, only to notice that 12–2 p.m. is blocked out, which is strange since it wasn't yesterday. Maybe Rob has grown tired of not having me to himself during set hours each day and decided to take over my lunch hour. I wouldn't put it past him.

I'm a nervous wreck for the rest of the morning, and unsure what to expect when I arrive at the assigned conference room at noon. What I don't expect is to find Dawson at the head of the table with a paper bag in hand.

"Did you block out my calendar during lunch, by chance?"

"I did." He takes out a gourmet sandwich, bottle of water, and cup of fruit, lining them up on the table. "Why didn't you tell me you were studying for the LSAT?" His gaze lingers on mine, waiting for an explanation.

I shift my weight from one foot to the other. "How do you know about that?" I say.

I haven't told anyone at the office. Most firms would view my plans to attend law school as a distraction or a lack of commitment since I'll have to quit at some point if I get accepted. I'd like to believe Dawson is different, but his ruthless approach to business makes me uncertain.

"You left your study guide on your desk yesterday."

Oh no.

I've been using my lunch breaks to study, but when Rob called me down to his office, I was in such a rush I forgot to put my book away. Rob would definitely take issue with my law school ambitions and claim that studying is a distraction from my work.

What if Dawson decides I'm not worth the effort and fires me?

I break into a cold sweat, my hands turning clammy at the thought. Dawson's influence could end my chances at law school with a single call. My chest tightens, each breath feeling shallower than the last. I try to inhale deeply, but the air doesn't seem to reach my lungs, causing me to wobble in my heels.

Dawson rushes to my side, catching me in his arms. "Easy there, Red." My arms naturally circle his neck, clinging to him like a lifeline. He carries me to the conference table, where he's set up the food and settles into a chair with me still cradled in his embrace.

His scent is calming, and I press my check against his neck to immerse myself in the heady aroma. He glances down at me as he gently cups my jaw with one hand, his thumb gliding lightly over my skin as if to reassure himself that I'm real. The tenderness in his touch and the heat radiating from his body overpower any guilt that what we're doing is wrong.

"When was the last time you ate?" he asks.

I stop to think for a minute. "Um… I had a cup of coffee on my way to the office."

He lets out a disapproving grunt. "That doesn't count." I watch as he unwraps a harvest veggie and goat cheese sandwich. "What were you planning to have for lunch?"

A bag of chips from the vending machine.

"I haven't thought that far ahead yet," I say, sticking with a safe answer.

"Are you hungry?"

The smell of fresh bread and herbs fills the air, making my stomach growl before I can respond.

Dawson chuckles. "Guess that's my answer." He positions

me so I'm facing the table and pushes the sandwich and fruit closer. "Eat."

"I'm not going to take your lunch."

He leans back in the chair, a smirk on his lips. "I ordered it for you."

"This is for me?" I wave a hand toward the delicious-looking meal.

"Yeah. You've been juggling a lot at work, so I wanted to help lighten your load. Now eat," he instructs.

At this point, the rational part of my brain kicks in, reminding me that I'm sitting on my boss's lap.

"I should probably sit in my own chair." Dawson's hand is resting on my thigh, but he doesn't make a move to remove it. "Anyone could walk in," I add.

Finding us in a compromising position would no doubt cause rumors.

Then why do I like it so much?

Dawson tightens his grip on my leg. "This is my private conference room. No one is going to interrupt us. Now eat," he repeats.

I swallow hard, weighing my options. The right thing to do would be to move. However, not only was his gesture of getting me lunch incredibly thoughtful, but a part of me is also tempted to stay where I am just for a little while longer.

He makes my decision easy when he pushes the sandwich toward me. It's a delightful blend of roasted vegetables and tangy goat cheese, each bite bursting with flavor, making me groan in satisfaction.

Dawson gazes at me with a tight expression, as if watching me eat is causing him physical pain. "Good?" he asks, his voice coming out husky.

"Delicious, thank you." I glance around, not seeing another sandwich. "Where's your lunch?"

"I'm meeting with a potential client at an Italian restaurant down the street later."

"Oh."

Most nights we work late, and he arranges for enough food to be delivered to feed a small army. At this rate, I'll have tried every fine dining restaurant in the city in the year, all from the comfort of the office. It's a stark contrast from Rob, who sends me on a wild goose chase every morning to get his breakfast, never permitting me to get anything for myself.

"At least let me pay you back," I say, and plop a grape into my mouth.

"Absolutely not," Dawson says, effectively shutting down my idea.

"But did you use a company card? Rob said that only partners are authorized to use it for meal expenses according to the employee handbook."

Dawson pinches the bridge of his nose. "Are you telling me when he makes you get him coffee and breakfast you don't get anything for yourself?" I shake my head, shifting my gaze to the ground. "I've had enough of that piece of shit," Dawson growls.

I place my hand on his arm. "It's not that big of a deal."

"It's a big fucking deal. He's lost his privilege to a company credit card." He takes a deep breath as he places his hand over mine. "I want to make one thing clear. You and the staff are *all* entitled to meals covered by the company. In fact, effective immediately, I'm giving everyone in the company a monthly stipend. I'll have HR issue a memo about it."

I give him a genuine smile. "That's very generous of you."

As I study his face, I notice something in his expression that I haven't seen before—a gentleness in his eyes, conveying a silent promise that I can always count on him.

Dawson Tate may come across as callous and unsympathetic, but I'm starting to see that beneath his tough exterior lies a heart of gold. He might not want anyone to know he cares, but his actions reveal the truth, showing a sense of compassion and respect.

My attention is drawn to the rose tattoo peeking out from under his shirt sleeve. He doesn't protest when I take his arm, rolling up the sleeve to his elbow, revealing the intricate sleeve of blackwork tattoos. "These really are beautiful. Did you design them?"

"I did," he says, a hint of pride in his eyes as he watches me admire his work.

I run my finger along the lines of the compass, thinking back to the night at Steel & Ink and his words about meaningful tattoos, and ask, "What does this one represent?"

"It's a constant reminder that I'm in charge of my own path and have the power to create any future I choose." He takes my finger in his and runs along the cardinal points of the tattoo. "Every direction symbolizes new opportunities. No matter which path I take, I'll achieve success because I determine the outcome."

"And to think I almost got a butterfly for my first tattoo because it was the first thing I thought of." I cover my mouth with my hand, laughing at how silly it would have been. "Thank god you talked me out of it."

He laughs softly. "Occasionally, I'm inclined to step in and save the day."

I give him a soft smile. "Why did you block out my calendar during lunch every day?" The question has been on my mind since he told me.

He places his hand on my knee, his grip still firm around my waist. "So you can study."

I glance at him. "Say that again."

"If you're going to score high on the LSAT, you need more time dedicated to studying. With the number of hours you're putting in at the firm, there's no way you're getting enough preparation."

He's not wrong. It doesn't help that I also have my job at the lounge club and an ever-expanding list of house projects.

I eye him warily. "What's the catch?"

He gives my hand a reassuring squeeze. "Can't a guy do something nice without being accused of ulterior motives?"

"Sure. When the person isn't you," I say, giving him a gentle jab in the chest. "From what I've witnessed, it's not like you to do something without expecting a significant payoff on your investment."

Dawson twirls a piece of my hair around his finger. "You're the exception," he whispers.

My heart skips a beat, hoping I heard him right. "Why?"

"Because if you want to become a lawyer, you deserve the chance to do it." His tone is sincere. "Although, I'm not sure you have what it takes to work in corporate law. You're way too nice."

I wrinkle my nose in disgust. "You couldn't pay me enough to do that. I may not have a definitive plan in place yet, but I do know that I'm going to work as a child advocacy lawyer someday."

Dawson's eyes visibly soften. "What made you decide that?"

"My mom passed away when I was a toddler, and I was lucky enough to be raised by my grandparents." I pause, reflecting on how their love shaped who I am today. "But so many kids grow up in foster care without anyone looking out for their best interests. I may not be able to help them all, but I'm going to make a difference for as many as I can."

"Well shit, you're making me look bad."

I knit my brows, perplexed. "That wasn't my intention," I assure him.

"Oh, I know." He offers a small smile. "I was in foster care until I was fifteen, and even though my adopted father is a public defender, I never considered working as a child advocate." He avoids my gaze as he plays with a strand of my hair. "I always wanted to be a partner at a corporate firm where I'd have control and the ability to dictate the terms of my success without limits."

My chest tightens at hearing a small piece of the challenges he faced as a kid. While I grew up without my parents, I was lucky to have been raised by two people who loved me unconditionally and provided me with a safe place to call home. I can't imagine what it must have been like for Dawson to be moved from one place to another, never knowing where he would end up.

His personality makes more sense to me now. I assume he's unwilling to get close to anyone because he's learned that most attachments only lead to disappointment or getting hurt.

I realize how much it means for him to open up, and I'm grateful that he trusts me enough to share this part of himself. Still, I refrain from making it a big deal, knowing he wouldn't welcome my sympathy.

"Don't worry," I say, patting him on the shoulder. "We can't all be selfless like me." I wink as I sit up in his lap to take a bite of my sandwich.

"You're right," he states. "You're one of a kind; the world could use more people like you."

With a few simple words, he makes me feel seen, and his un-expected tenderness has me sinking deeper into his embrace. His commanding presence, the low rumble of his voice, and the way his piercing gaze seems to see right through me. His commanding presence, the low rumble of his voice, and the way his piercing gaze seems to see right through me is proof how easily

I put my sandwich down and take a sip of water.

"Thanks for lunch, I really appreciate it."

"You're welcome." Dawson replies.

My body still when he reaches out to brush a crumb from the corner of my mouth, his thumb lingering against my lower lip.

"Maybe I should get up now," I whisper.

Dawson drops his hand. "If you want to."

When I don't move to get out of his lap he brings his hand to the small of my back, trailing his fingers along the fabric of my shirt in a hypnotic fashion. My breath catching when he leans in to tuck my hair behind my ear, pressing a chaste kiss to my temple. He exhales slowly, the air brushing against the side of my face, and a soft moan escapes my lips.

"You're so beautiful, Red," he says softly.

His words of affection cause goosebumps to rise on my arms.

He gently grips the base of my neck and moves forward to brush his nose against mine. His touch is soft, almost reverent, as if he's imprinting this moment in his memory. A whimper escapes me when he tilts his head to nip at my bottom lip.

"Fuck, your sweetness is intoxicating," he says quietly.

I gasp when he seals his mouth to mind. Our electric kiss creates a fire inside me, leaving me craving more.

When I shift in Dawson's lap, my eyes widening as my ass brushes against his cock, and I can't help but break our kiss to glance down to see the evidence of how I affect him.

Unable to contain my curiosity, I tentatively move my hand between us to rest against his slacks. My breath hitches when I feel the outline of where his cock is pressing against the fabric. A guttural groan passes his lips when I move my fingers in a circular motion, teasing him.

"We can't do more than kiss," I whisper.

"I'd never dream of it," he smirks.

He places my hand over his and pushes our joined fingers firmly against his hard on. "Feel what you do to me, Red."

Just as my mouth parts for another kiss, his phone goes off, jolting me back to reality.

"Dammit," he mutters.

I squeak in surprise, scrambling from his lap.

As my haze of desire dissipates, I'm acutely aware that my body was just plastered against his and that we kissed. No, we were doing much more than that. We were fucking with our mouths while I traced his dick with my hand in a conference room in broad daylight.

Oh god, we're in so much trouble.

We're supposed to be keeping things strictly professional, and what just happened was the exact opposite.

Without a second thought, I bolt toward the door.

"Reese, where are you going?" Dawson calls out as he stands, his voice a mix of concern and desire.

"Back to work," I say, making sure not to look back, too embarrassed to let him see my flushed face.

I've never felt more conflicted. On one hand, I'm embarrassed for letting things go so far. I only have myself to blame since I'm the one who practically pounced on him, allowing my lust to overshadow any potential consequences. On the other hand, I can't deny being back in his arms felt like that was where I was meant to be.

The worst part is, if things go south, not only is my job at stake, but I have a sneaking suspicion that losing Dawson would be equally, if not more devastating.

CHAPTER 11

Dawson

REESE HAS DOMINATED MY THOUGHTS SINCE WE GAVE IN to temptation yesterday. Who am I kidding? She hasn't been far from my mind since the day I met her. The kiss we shared in the conference room was like a shot of top-shelf brandy, and I'm craving another taste. We've both avoided the topic, keeping things strictly businesslike, and I'm careening toward the edge.

I've done everything to control my wandering thoughts, but it's a losing battle when we're together. Like this morning, when she leaned over my desk to review a document, and a fantasy took hold in my mind that's played on repeat since.

I lock the door to my office and stride toward Reese, a determined glint in my eye. With her attention still on the documents in front of her, I wind my arm around her waist, peppering kisses along her neck. She lets out a low moan when I nibble on her ear, her fingernail digging into my arm.

Unable to hold out any longer, I spin her around to face me before sweeping my hand across the desk, sending everything scattering to the floor.

I lift her into my arms and hoist her onto the wooden surface. Her heated gaze is locked on mine as I hike up her skirt, bunching it around her waist and exposing her black lace underwear. She lifts her hips and I drag the thin scrap of material down her legs, tucking it into my pocket for safekeeping.

Not willing to waste a second, I drop to my knees, my head aligned with her core. I hitch her leg over my shoulder and kiss along her smooth skin. My hands spread her quivering thighs and I lick her pussy in long, steady strokes. When I glance up, she has a wanton expression on her face as I plunge three fingers inside her tight cunt. I work her clit hard, telling her to be a good girl and come for me as her slender fingers tangle in my hair. She arches her back when she comes, shouting my name, without a care for who hears her sounds of pleasure.

I'm snapped from my fantasy when my phone vibrates on my desk.

Fuck.

I glance around and sigh in relief when I find I'm still alone in my office. My cock is rock-hard, and I take a minute to readjust myself. It's late Thursday afternoon, and I hate the idea of spending yet another weekend without seeing Reese. God, my obsession with her is getting out of hand.

When my phone buzzes again, I'm grateful for the distraction.

Harrison: Hey.

Harrison: You free to grab a drink tomorrow night?

Dawson: Sure.

Harrison: I'll text you the address.

Dawson: We're not meeting at the bar?

Harrison: Not this time.

Dawson: Fine, but it better not be a club.

After ten minutes with no reply, I send another message.

Dawson: You better be in a board meeting and not ignoring me.

Dawson: If that address is for a club, you're buying two rounds for everyone there.

Damn it. I should have told him I was busy. I toss my phone down and when I glance out my open door, I find Reese heading toward her desk.

This may be the only chance I have to speak to her before the weekend, and I'm not about to give that up.

"Reese, can you come here for a second?" I call out.

A few seconds later, she strides in with a pen tucked behind her ear, balancing a coffee cup in one hand and a stack of files in the other.

"What's up?" she asks, coming to stand next to my desk.

"Can you send me the updated Irving contract? I need to have multiple copies for Wes's team to review when I get to their office tomorrow."

"You know, there's this fancy thing called a chat system? Or you could just text me if the first option is too much trouble." She says with a playful smirk.

Then I wouldn't get to see your beautiful face.

"Why message when your desk is right outside my door?"

"I left five copies for you this morning. They're tabbed and ready to go." She motions to a stack of folders that I pushed off to the side earlier.

A frown mars my face. "Oh, okay. Thanks."

Reese spins towards the door, ready to leave, but stops when she hears my voice. "Can you call Villa Napoli and confirm that the catering order will be delivered at Irving Tower tomorrow at 12:30 p.m.?" I ask.

She glances over her shoulder. "I did it this morning. They'll have two servers there to assist in setting everything up."

"One more thing," I say before she can bolt.

She turns to face me, clutching her coffee for dear life. "What is it?"

My mind draws a blank, scrambling to find an excuse to get her to stay. "Umm... I think my printer is out of black ink. Can you get me a new cartridge from the break room?"

She sighs, and puts a hand on her hip. "Dawson, I saw you change both cartridges last week." *Damn, I forgot about that.* "As much as I'd love to humor your little game, I have a lot of work to get through today. So, unless there's anything else...?" She lets the question hang in the air.

I should say something, but I'm distracted by the neckline of her shirt, dipping slightly to reveal a hint of cleavage and a dark green bra. My thoughts drift again to our moment in my conference room, remembering the feel of her nestled in my lap with my hands gripping her hips as I kissed her with no regard for the consequences.

Reese's voice snaps me out of my daydream. "Dawson?"

When I glance up, her gaze is bouncing between me and the door.

"I'm sorry, what did you say?" I ask.

She lets out an exasperated sigh. "Was that all you wanted?"

"Just wanted to remind you I'll be out of the office tomorrow."

"Yes. You've mentioned it several times."

I run a hand through my already disheveled hair. "That's right."

Her gaze softens, worry clouding her expression. "Are you okay?"

I wave her off, embarrassed that I'm acting like a teenager with a crush. "I'm fine. You can go."

"Okay," she says, and the smile she gives me brightens the room.

The door clicks behind her when she leaves, and I bury my face in my hands. What the hell is wrong with me? I pride myself on being in control and self-assured, but with Reese, it feels like I'm stumbling through uncharted territory without any sense of direction.

"The next time you drag me to a club, you'll owe me another favor," I mutter.

"Yeah, whatever," Harrison says, clearly distracted as he scans the room.

He failed to mention we'd be meeting at a crowded lounge bar with a live jazz band and a drink menu dedicated to signature cocktails. True to my word, I told the bartender that Harrison was covering two rounds of drinks for everyone in the club. Surprisingly, Harrison handed over his card without protest.

Patrons are seated in plush armchairs and velvet sectionals under dim lighting, enjoying their appetizers and fruity drinks. I much prefer the dive bar in Brooklyn, where the alcohol is simple and there's a relaxed atmosphere with fewer people.

Several women openly gawk at us as we pass, their eyes lingering with clear interest. I pay them no mind as I follow Harrison. There's only one woman I'm interested in taking home tonight, and she's not here.

If she were here right now, I'd say fuck the rules and drag her to the nearest corner and kiss her until she couldn't think straight.

I almost crash into Harrison when he stops abruptly. "A bit of warning would have been nice," I mutter.

"Sorry," he says, his gaze shifting toward a group of women climbing a spiral staircase.

He's acting strange tonight. Given what I know about him, he's not the kind of guy to openly check out women or hang out in a glitzy club.

"What are we really doing here?" I ask.

"There's a catered VIP party on the second floor," he says.

I shoot him a questioning look. "Since when are you into parties?"

He grits his teeth. "I'm not."

Harrison heads for the stairs, not waiting for a reply. I follow, intrigued by what has him so preoccupied. When we get to the second floor, a hostess with short black hair and a tailored black suit is waiting with a tablet in hand.

"Good evening, gentlemen." She offers us a sultry smile. "May I have your names, please?"

Harrison doesn't seem to hear her, his entire focus on surveying the room.

"Dawson Tate and Harrison Stafford," I tell the hostess, slipping her a hundred-dollar bill.

She makes a show of checking the guest list before waving us through. "Thank you, Mr. Tate. I hope you both have a lovely evening."

I study Harrison with concern as he aimlessly wanders the room, weaving in between patrons and tables. His usual composure is nowhere to be found, I'd find it amusing if it weren't so disconcerting.

After he nearly collides with two different servers carrying drinks, I place a hand on his shoulder to stop him.

Harrison turns around, frowning. "What?" he snaps.

"Why don't you tell me who we're looking for so I can help."

The sooner we find this mystery person, the sooner I can get the hell out of here.

He sighs. "Her name's Fallon, and she's catering this event," he says, motioning around the room.

"And why are we stalking this Fallon person?"

"We're not," he says. "She just moved here from London and doesn't know how dangerous the city can be. I just want to make sure she's not being sweet-talked by some hedge fund manager into going home with him so he can show her his state-of-the-art kitchen."

"That's oddly specific," I note. "But I'm sure she can manage on her own. She's from London, and I'm guessing she's used to navigating a big city and knows how to avoid unwanted advances." Harrison shoots me a scowl, and I hold my hands up defensively. "Okay then. Why don't we go back and ask the hostess if she…" I trail off when a flash of red catches my eye from across the room before disappearing into the sea of people.

My pulse quickens as I crane my neck, searching the crowd. *Why are there so many people standing around?*

Harrison's voice cuts through my focus. "Now you're the one acting strange."

I dismiss him with a wave and take a step forward, my gaze still roaming the area. Then, I catch another glimpse of red, the woman coming into full view, and my heart races with recognition.

It's Reese.

She's in the far corner of the room, wearing a black cocktail dress with a plunging neckline that hugs her curves and falls just above her knees. A smile tugs at my lips when I notice her sneakers—black with intricate, hand-drawn white-and-gold flowers.

My smile fades when a man comes to stand next to her. He's tall and lanky with short brown hair and stubble on his face. He looks to be in his early twenties. A red haze clouds my vision and my jaw ticks as I watch him lean in to tuck a strand of hair behind Reese's ear. He says something that causes her to laugh, and the musical sound is like a magnet, drawing me closer.

My patience snaps when the man has the nerve to put his hand on Reese's lower back and hands her a bottle of water.

"I'll be back," I tell Harrison, not bothering to elaborate.

I move across the club with determination, oblivious to the other partygoers who give me a wide berth as I pass. When I get closer, I can hear Reese talking. "You're the best, Noah. Thanks for this." She takes a long drink from the water.

"Anytime, babe. Now shouldn't you be getting back to work?" he says with a smug grin.

That's when I notice the serving tray tucked under Reese's arm.

What the hell is she doing working at a club?

Better question, why did he just call her babe?

"Shouldn't you be doing the same?" she asks with a mischievous glint in her eye.

"I had to come over and make sure you were staying hydrated. Now, finish your water," Noah says.

"Yes, *boss*," Reese quips.

"I thought that title only belonged to me?" I cut in, my tone cold.

Her eyes widen with recognition at the sound of my voice, and her gaze shifts in my direction, holding the bottle halfway to her lips.

"D-Dawson?" she stammers, her cheeks turning red. "What are you doing here?"

Noah positions himself close to Reese as if to shield her.

"Dawson Tate," I tell him, extending my hand.

He relaxes his stance when he hears my name and accepts my handshake. I give him a firm grip, establishing my dominance.

"I've heard so much about you. I'm a court clerk for the New York County Supreme Court. You're kind of a legend there." He chuckles nervously.

"I see. And how exactly do you know Reese?"

"We met during our freshman year in college. We've been friends ever since, and both of us work here. We're also studying for the LSAT together."

"I'm a server here," Reese chimes in, holding up the empty tray. "And Noah's a bartender."

My mind reels at this information. Why didn't she mention she had another job? Does she go home with Noah after their shift? Are they sleeping together? A flood of questions race through my mind as my gaze darts between them.

It never crossed my mind that Reese could be seeing someone. Now, all the logical questions I had pushed aside are suddenly pressing.

"Reese, can we talk somewhere in private?" I ask, tamping down my jealousy and the overwhelming urge to get her out of her.

The last thing I should do is make a scene, but I can't wait to talk to her.

She glances at her watch, then back at me. "I have ten minutes until my break is over. We can use the office upstairs." She turns to Noah and hands him her water bottle. "Let Lacy know I'll be back soon."

He gives her an affectionate smile. "Absolutely."

"Thanks, I won't be long," she promises.

Reese looks back at me, her eyes stormy. She grabs my arm, tugging me toward the kitchen area. That's when I spot Harrison engaged in a heated argument with a short blond woman wearing a chef's apron. She's standing with a hand on her hip and has a finger jabbed into his chest. This must be Fallon, and she seems far from happy to see Harrison.

I turn back to Reese when she tugs me through a side door and up another flight of stairs, ushering me inside an office *Management* embossed on the door. A large wooden desk and an office chair are situated in one corner, across from a leather couch. The walls are decorated with a series of jazz-inspired art pieces, and there are floor-to-ceiling windows overlooking the club.

As soon as Reese shuts the door, I stalk toward her.

"Are you dating Noah?" It slips out before I can stop it, not that I would have anyway. I've learned from experience that straightforward questions are the most effective way to get the answers I want.

Reese chews on her lower lip as she eyes me with suspicion. "That's not something you're allowed to ask an employee."

I shrug. "Since we're off the clock, I'd say it's fair game. Now stop stalling and answer the question."

Reese huffs in frustration. "Noah is my best friend, not that I owe you an explanation."

"Tell me, Red, do all of your friends call you babe?"

She shakes her head. "Just Noah."

"Are you interested in him?"

She rolls her eyes. "I'm not, and for the record, even if I were, you're more his type than I am."

A wave of relief washes over me at hearing that she's not interested in Noah. My shoulders relax and I smirk. "Is that so?"

Reese folds her arms across her chest, glaring at me. "Yes. Now that you've had a chance to interrogate me, it's my turn," she challenges. "What are *you* doing here? Taking a break from the tattoo parlor to find a hookup for the night?" I don't miss her biting tone.

"Now who's jealous?" I taunt. "I came here with a client. We usually meet at a dive bar in Brooklyn, but a woman he knows is catering an event here tonight and he wanted to see her."

"You don't strike me as someone who does business in dive bars."

"I don't. I'm not representing Harrison right now."

"So, he's your friend?"

"No, he's a client." She furrows her brow like she doesn't understand. "Care to explain why you're waitressing on a Friday night instead of studying and getting a good night's sleep?" I ask, changing the subject.

She scoffs. "No. I reviewed the employee handbook before accepting my position at Thompson & Tate. There's no policy against having a second job, as long as it doesn't overlap with my scheduled hours and isn't with a direct competitor."

There should be.

It bothers me that she's been juggling two jobs and wearing herself down in the process. I have half a mind to call the HR director and have them insert a clause prohibiting outside employment immediately. But then I'd have to explain why I'm at a club with an employee on the weekend and why I'm so concerned about her having a second job. Regrettably, the handbook does include a policy against fraternization with employees. I should have HR change that too.

Hell, we should toss the whole damn thing out the window.

That's not a thought a lawyer would usually entertain, but this woman is making me think irrationally and all I want to do is hold her in my arms again.

"Dawson, please say something," she pleads.

"I don't want you working here," I say bluntly.

She appears briefly flustered but quickly recovers, putting her hands on her hips and says, "Too bad. Your control doesn't extend past your office. You don't get to tell me what to do when I'm not at work."

I grunt as I walk toward her, my voice low. "And what if I want to?"

Her breathing quickens with every step I take. "Want to what?"

I wind my arm around her waist and use my other hand to sweep a loose strand of hair from her face. "Have a say in what you do outside the office," I confess.

Her eyes flutter closed like she's savoring my touch. Her instinctive reaction gives me a sense of satisfaction; I like that I'm not the only one who's affected by our proximity.

When Reese opens her eyes, she places her hand on my chest as if torn between drawing me in and pushing me away. "I hate to break it to you, but you don't always get what you want." She says, her hand still lingering.

I place mine over hers, savoring the warmth of her touch. "I'm just worried you're going to spread yourself too thin."

"I'm perfectly capable of handling things on my own," she reminds me.

"There's no doubt about that," I say with a smile. "But that doesn't mean you have to. In case you haven't noticed, you're important to me, Red."

"I am?"

"Yes, you are."

A mischievous smile crosses her face. "You're not the only one who should get to go around calling the shots, Mr. Tate," she murmurs. "I'd like a say in things too."

I tilt my head, amused. "Just say the word and you can call the shots whenever you want."

Her eyes widen for a split second before she masks her reaction. "In that case… Dawson?"

Fuck, I love it when she says my name.

"Yeah, Red?"

She rises on her toes, her lips mere inches from mine. "I'd like you to kiss me." She leans closer. "Please."

I thought she'd never ask.

"Damn, I like it when you're sweet."

I cup her chin and crash my mouth to hers. When I finally pull back, she gasps for air. I walk her backward until she is pinned to glass with her back facing the club., her eyes locked on me. I'm tired of dancing around the undeniable fact that I want Reese, and I have every intention of giving her a taste of what it would be like to spend a night with me.

She bites her bottom lip and whispers, "Why did you stop?"

"Close your eyes."

"Daws—"

"Do you trust me?"

Despite her initial reluctance, she nods.

I press a kiss on her forehead. "Now close your eyes," I repeat.

She does as I ask and leans her head against the wall, placing her hands at her side.

"Good girl."

She lets out a shuddered breath in response.

"You like it when I call you my good girl, don't you?"

"Maybe." A teasing grin plays on her lips.

With delicate precision, I trace her angelic face, my fingers trailing across her forehead, moving to her right cheekbone, then her left. My exploration continues, gliding across her freckled nose then running the pad of my thumb across her pouty lips.

I watch the rise and fall of Reese's chest, noting the quickening of her breath when I continue my path down the column of her neck. A surge of satisfaction courses through me, fully aware that I'm responsible for her heightened response.

"Have I told you how beautiful you are?" I murmur in her ear.

Her eyes flutter open, and I'm mesmerized by the depth of her emerald gaze. "You're not so bad yourself when you're not being a tyrant."

Reese tilts her head back to look at me, and when she smiles, I'm a goner. She winds her arms around my neck, drawing me closer.

I cup her face with my hands, pressing kisses along her jawline. When I get to her mouth, I trace my tongue along her plump bottom lip in teasing strokes. She lets out a soft moan as her tongue meets mine, and she pulls me closer. When she tugs my lip between her teeth, our connection turns from tentative exploration to wild and frenzied.

I grind my cock against her core, and she pushes against me in response. Our moans fill the air as I explore her mouth with fervor.

It's a fucking turn-on to witness her uninhibited side

first-hand. When she cries out for more, I bunch up the material of her dress and shove it out of the way. I hike her leg around my waist, placing my other hand securely on her hip. When she grips my hair, it sparks a fuse inside me.

"No more waiting, Red." I step back, and spin her around so she's facing the glass wall, overlooking the club. "Look out the window," I whisper as I wind my arm around her waist.

Reese is panting as she follows my order, her eyes darting to the people below. Her breath hitches when I push her panties aside and tease at her entrance before sinking two fingers inside her. "Damn, you're soaked. Is this all for me?"

"Oh, Dawson," she whimpers.

I lean forward, running my tongue along the column of her neck, leaving kisses and gentle bites along her collarbone.

When I add a third finger, Reese lets out a strangled sound of arousal. It's the most sensual sound I've ever heard, making me want this—want *her*—even more.

Her hands are pressed against the glass as I move my fingers. Her back is arched, her ass rubbing against my cock. I wrap my free hand around her neck and tilt her head to capture her mouth in mine.

"Are you going to come on my hand with a crowd down there? Anyone could be watching." I murmur against her lips.

She looks forward, clenching tighter around my fingers as I speak.

Looks like my Red might be an exhibitionist, although there's no chance of that happening tonight. I noticed earlier that the windows are made of one-sided glass, but it turns me on watching Reese's reaction to the idea that someone could be watching.

"Oh my god, don't stop," she breathes out.

"Not until you come like a good girl," I promise.

I'm hard as a rock as I watch Reese unravel before me. I can sense that she's close to the edge, her body coiling tighter with each plunge of my fingers. I strum her clit with my thumb, and within seconds she shatters around my hand. She rests the back of her head on my chest and lets out a strangled cry of pleasure. She doesn't stop riding my hand until I've wrung every drop of desire from her core.

Reese is utterly captivating when she's on the verge of release but watching her come is something else entirely.

"That's my girl," I praise.

I bring my fingers to my mouth, sucking them clean. Reese bites her lip, watching me with rapture. I flash her a wicked grin as I groan, relishing the taste of her essence on my tongue. She doesn't take her eyes off me as she reaches down to massage my cock through my pants, but I shake my head.

"What about you?" she asks.

"This was about *you*." I gently stroke her jaw before reaching down to smooth out her dress.

Giving her pleasure brings me a sense of fulfillment, and makes me feel closer to her.

"I've decided listening to you come is my new favorite sound," I grin.

Reese blinks at me, as though she's just coming out of a trance. The realization of what we've done registering.

She places her hands over her head. "Oh my god. I can't believe I just let my boss finger me in the office of a club while I'm supposed to be working. It was a lapse in judgment, that's all," she rushes out. "I got caught up in the moment when you called me a good girl." A blush creeps across her cheeks at the admission. "And then you looked at me with that ridiculous smoldering gaze of yours, and I fell under your spell."

Have I mentioned how adorable she is when she rambles.

She holds her hand up to stop me when I try to get closer. "We should pretend this didn't happen. Every time we cross this line, we're putting our careers at risk."

I'd like to tell her she's wrong and convince her to admit what just happened between us meant something to her. But she's already nervous, and I can't risk losing her because of my selfish desires.

"I have to get back to work," she says abruptly.

"Woah, hold on." I take her by the hand. "We haven't talked about why you're working here."

What I'd like to do is demand she quit and haul her ass out of here. However, she'd probably leave the firm and work here full-time just to spite me.

"That's not your problem," she retorts.

I bring her fingers up to my lips. "I hate to break it to you, Red, but the taste of you on my tongue makes it my problem."

I don't miss the catch in her breath. "Can we talk about this later? I really do have to get back."

I run my hand through my hair, willing myself not to over-react. I'm used to getting my way, but Reese has a way of turning my plans upside at every turn.

"Fine, but this isn't over," I state.

She pauses near the door. "Goodbye, Dawson." she says softly before leaving the office.

With anyone else, I would have been content with what just happened. Now that I know what it feels like to have Reese wrapped in my arms—to make her come—I'm already plotting ways to make it happen again.

Before today, she's been quick to rush out of a room after one of our interactions. Which leaves me with a glimmer of hope that things between us are moving forward—toward what?

I don't know. But I'm willing to take the risk for Reese.

CHAPTER 12

Reese

THE MOMENT DAWSON AND I SHARED AT THE CLUB STILL lives rent-free in my mind a week later. It was *the* hottest sexual experience I've had thus far. I didn't care that a thin glass wall was the only thing that separated us from hundreds of people. I was done for the second Dawson called me his *good girl*.

I don't have a rational explanation for my impulsive behavior, but Dawson brings out a side of me that I didn't know existed. When I'm with him I feel bold and free to speak my mind without fear of judgment. We're straddling a fine line, pushing our professional boundaries and truth be told, I've never felt more alive.

What happened at the club was like lighting a matchstick in a tinderbox, setting a blazing inferno to the delicate balance of control I've been holding on to.

Seeing him there sent a course of jealousy through my veins. The idea of him cozying up to another woman and flirting or having a meaningful conversation bothers me.

It doesn't help that part of me has wanted to kiss him again since the night at the tattoo shop, and once his mouth was on mine again, I couldn't find it in me to stop him from going further. Images of him gazing at me with those bright blue eyes as he traces my jawline torment me. His scent lingers on the dress I wore that night—a reminder that it happened.

It's another late night at the office, and I should be responding to emails, but I've been staring at my computer for the past half hour. Today has dragged from all the tedious tasks Rob has asked me to do.

The elevator's chime catches my attention, and the same courier from the first night Dawson had food delivered comes down the hall.

Dawson exits his office with his hands in his pockets, watching the guy like a hawk.

The courier is careful not to glance my way when he hands Dawson the bag.

"Good to see you're on time tonight," Dawson says, passing him a hundred-dollar tip.

"Thank you, sir," the courier says, pocketing the cash as he walks back to the elevator.

Dawson may be abrasive, but he recognizes and rewards those who deliver results.

"You still avoiding me?" Dawson asks as he passes by my desk.

I shift in my chair, glancing at the ground. "I'm not avoiding you," I whisper.

He leans his hip against my desk, a little smirk playing on his lips. "Sure you aren't."

Okay, maybe I have tried to keep my distance. It's been easier than expected, given that he's been spending more of his time at Wes Irving's office than at the firm over the past week.

However, true to his word, my calendar remains blocked out every day from 12–2 for me to study in his private conference room. When I arrive, there's always a gourmet meal and a bottle of water waiting for me. Having a quiet space to prepare for the LSAT is such a relief. His kind gestures are another reason why I'm drawn to him.

Now that he's here with me, I'm struck by how much I've missed him—though I'm certainly not going to admit it out loud.

At first glance, we have little in common. He's a brooding thirty-five-year-old lawyer and the owner of a tattoo shop. I'm a twenty-three-year-old paralegal struggling to make ends meet, with a crumbling old house for a home, and a love for playing bingo with a group of merciless senior citizens.

A chance meeting brought us together, but now it feels like our chemistry is too difficult to ignore. Beyond my initial mortification that he caught me working there, I'm sure he's wondering why when I have a good job at Thompson & Tate.

I can't afford to rack up student loans like others do, so I'm taking the slower, more practical approach to reach my goals. I made peace with it a long time ago, but I don't want to be judged by those who might not understand the choices I've made.

"If you're not avoiding me, then come eat with me," he says as he goes into his office.

Against my better judgment, I get up from my desk, lingering in his doorway with my arms crossed against my chest. Dawson holds out a takeout container, inviting me to join him on the couch. "Please," he adds when I don't move.

Whatever he ordered smells delicious, and my rumbling stomach reminds me it's been a few hours since I had lunch.

"I could eat," I say, eyeing the takeout.

"Thought you might," he says, his amusement evident in his expression.

Once I'm seated, I open the box and am welcomed by the mouthwatering scent of shepherd's pie. It's filled with ground beef, diced carrots, peas, and a cheesy layer of mashed potatoes.

This is my favorite dish, one my grandma used to make every

week. I haven't had it since she moved to Oak Ridge, so it's been a while.

He remembered.

Dawson frowns when he notices I haven't touched my dinner. "Everything okay with your food?"

"It looks perfect," I say, unwrapping the fork that came with the meal. "It just hit me how long it's been since I've had Shepherd's pie, that's all."

Dawson purses his lips as he bites into his bacon and mushroom burger. Once he swallows, he says, "I wanted to do something nice for you because I see how hard you work and how rarely you make yourself a priority."

There are moments when I wish he didn't have such a powerful effect on me, but his thoughtful gestures make it hard to ignore when they're in stark contrast with his treatment of others. He refuses to spare anyone's feelings, especially when a crucial case is on the line, and remains unbothered when he's ruined their lives. Which makes his behavior with me all the more perplexing.

"I appreciate it. This food is delicious," I say.

We eat in comfortable silence, and I enjoy every bite of my shepherd's pie.

When Dawson finishes his meal, he tosses his empty takeout container into the paper bag and turns to face me. "Are you ready to tell me why you're working at Echo?"

I was hoping he'd drop it, but I should have known better.

After swallowing my last bite of food, I dispose of my container before responding. "I need the extra money, and the tips at the club are generous."

Waitressing isn't something I'm ashamed of; it's made it possible to make ends meet while saving for law school, and I'm proud of my hard work. Still, I worry he won't understand my motive, given the paralegals at his firm earn well above the industry standard.

"Can I ask you what you need the money for?" he asks.

I shift in my seat, refusing to meet his gaze. "It's not anything illegal if that's what you're thinking," I say with a hint of sarcasm. "There are just some extra bills I have to take care of. That's all."

Oak Ridge is one of the priciest assisted living facilities in the area, but Grams loves the staff and has several friends who live there. She spent her whole life working and raising me. Now it's my turn to make sure she's well taken care of.

Dawson furrows his brow, seemingly unsatisfied with my answer. "I wish you'd tell me more," he says, placing his hand on my knee. "But I understand why you'd prefer to keep some things to yourself for now."

My mind fixates on the last two words: *for now*. It feels like a promise that he'll be here when I'm ready to share more. Whether I'm misinterpreting it or not, it brings me comfort knowing that he's here for me. Aside from Noah and Grams, I don't have anyone else in my corner who I trust implicitly, and there's a part of me who wishes more than anything that Dawson could be another person I could rely on.

"Thanks. I admit it can be lonely at times." The admission slips out unbidden.

Dawson doesn't hesitate to lift my chin with his hand, coaxing me to meet his earnest gaze. "I know the feeling all too well," he murmurs.

His gentle touch, and the rare glimpse into his own vulnerability, offer me an unexpected sense of calm.

When my eyes land on his mouth, there's a sudden shift in the air. I catch myself licking my lips. This is dangerous territory, especially considering we're in his office, but I'd give anything for a brief escape—from mounting bills, endless responsibilities, and the moral dilemma of my growing feelings for my boss.

It all fades when he leans forward, our faces mere inches apart, and the sound of our intermingled breathing fills the room.

It takes every scrap of willpower not to close the distance between us. We're in uncharted waters, and it feels like we're on the brink of something... Something that could change everything. If I surrender to my feelings, it could take us past the point of no return. Yet, as I look at Dawson, I can't help but think that the right might be worth taking.

Like he can sense my indecision, he scoots closer, wraps an arm around my waist, and tugs me to his side. "No more running, angel," he whispers, tipping my chin. "I'm going to kiss you now."

His bold declaration ignites my desire, emboldening me to take the lead.

"Not if I kiss you first," I murmur, bridging the last bit of space between us.

Taken aback by my daring gesture, he blinks momentarily before his fingers slide into my hair and he deepens our kiss. Lost in the magic of the moment, I place my hands on his shoulders.

"You taste so damn sweet, Red," he groans into my mouth.

Our kiss is electric, igniting a fire inside me that has me craving more.

Dawson holds me like he never wants to let me go, and part of me hopes he never does. Which is why I'm caught off guard when he suddenly pulls away, leaving me dazed.

"What's wrong?" I breathe.

"Nothing," he insists, gliding his thumb along the curve of my lip like he's having second thoughts. "But you've been avoiding me since the night at the club, and I don't want to overstep any boundaries you've set since then," he says. "You're too important for me to risk doing anything to make you uncomfortable."

A shiver runs through me at the sincerity in his voice.

"I appreciate the sentiment, but are you forgetting I'm the one who initiated the kiss?" I shift closer so our thighs are touching, eliminating the space he put between us when he broke the kiss. "When have I done anything I don't want to do?" I ask, resting my hand on his.

Dawson gives me a pointed look. "For starters, you're forced to work with me despite declining my offer, and you had to move floors because of me. If I remember correctly, that wasn't something you wanted either."

He's not wrong.

At first, I didn't want to work with Dawson to avoid speculation from our co-workers about the new girl getting preferential treatment. However, that only played a small part. The main reason I told him no was because I knew how visceral my reactions to him could be. Our first kiss laid bare the passion between us, which has only intensified with every heated glance, lingering touch, and playful exchange.

Dawson runs his thumb along the back of my hand, his eyes on mine. "You're so damn beautiful, it's almost painful." He pauses briefly, exhaling slowly. "My office door is open, and anyone could have walked in on us." A flush rises to my cheeks when I glance over to see that he's right. "It's difficult to think clearly when we're together." He admits.

I mentally scold myself for being so careless. It's late, and everyone on our floor is gone for the night, but that's beside the point. It would only take one person to see us for the fallout to be catastrophic. Irreparable, even.

I move my hands to my lap, running my hands across my skirt pleats, thinking about the consequences if we'd been caught tonight. I'm not naive enough to think Dawson would face as many repercussions if our secret got out. It always comes down to the one with the most to lose, which, in this case, is me.

Dawson isn't the only one who's not thinking rationally.

No matter how often I promise to maintain professional boundaries, we always end up caught in a perpetual loop of sexual tension and unresolved feelings.

"Where do we go from here?" I say, hoping he has a solution.

"I wish there was an easy answer," he admits. "If I were a better man, I'd do the sensible thing and keep things strictly business moving forward." A knot forms in my stomach, afraid he's about to walk away from me. "But honestly, I'm not sure if I can do that. Can you?" I slowly shake my head. "We have to decide if this"—he motions between us—"is worth pursuing, consequences be damned. Because if we find ourselves in a situation like this again with no chance of being interrupted, I plan to do far more than just kiss you."

I press my legs together as images from our encounter at the club flit through my mind. It was fueled by lust and forbidden desires. If we had let it go on any further, it could have left us both tangled in a web of regret, further complicating things. Adding the kiss we just shared to the mix, it's obvious we've crossed a line that can't be uncrossed. It could lead to a new chapter and have serious ramifications for both my heart and career.

Begging the question: Is the risk worth the reward, or will the potential consequences threaten the possibility of a chance at something real?

CHAPTER 13

Dawson

REESE LEFT MY OFFICE TWO HOURS AGO, AND I HAVEN'T managed to get a single thing done apart from pace the room. It doesn't sit right with me that we left things unresolved. I'm usually the guy with a solution for any situation, and it's frustrating that this time, I'm at a loss about what to do next.

It took every ounce of willpower to pull away from our kiss. Reese's mouth tasted like sweet temptation, and when she brought her lips to mine, it reassured me that she wants me as much as I want her. Yet, as soon as her body molded to mine, the worry crept in that I could cause her more harm than good.

I'm her boss, for crying out loud. If anyone should be listening to common sense, it's me.

With Reese, that's easier said than done.

My mind is a chaotic mess, so I call the person who's helped me navigate my most difficult challenges.

"Hi honey." Martha's voice sounds groggy when she answers the phone.

"I'm sorry. Did I wake you?" I ask.

"Colby left a few hours ago to go to the local booking facility to meet a client. I tried waiting up for him but fell asleep on the couch watching *Only Murders in the Building*. It's a good thing you called. Any longer and I would have had a stiff neck for days."

I chuckle. "Happy I could help save you from a chiropractic disaster."

"Would you like to tell me what's bothering you?"

I take a seat on the edge of my desk, drumming my fingers against the polished wood. "What makes you think something's wrong? Can't I just call to check in?"

"Of course you can, but you're *my* son." Her voice softens. "It's my job to know when you're not okay, whether you tell me or not."

When Colby and Martha adopted me, I didn't feel comfortable calling them mom and dad. Those terms are tainted by the memory of a birth mother who abandoned me and a nameless man who never bothered to be involved in my life. Colby and Martha mean so much more to me than that. They provided me with the stability and the love of a family I never thought I'd have.

Although I avoid parental terms, I've never objected to being called their son. It's a reflection of the strong bond we've built. The sense of belonging and support they've given me.

"Dawson, I can't help you unless you tell me what's on your mind," Martha says, the sound of the TV humming in the background

"It's nothing."

That's a lie.

"Why don't you tell me anyway?" Martha encourages.

One thing's for sure—she's never been one to shy away from helping me, even if I'm not the most receptive. I've come to appreciate her unwavering determination and am grateful to have someone who cares enough to stand by me even when I'm being stubborn.

I rub the back of my neck, considering what to share about Reese. "A few months ago, a woman came into the tattoo shop to hide from an awkward first date." A small smile crosses my face as I remember seeing Reese for the first time. Her pouty lips parted as she breathed heavily, her red hair cascading around her face in wild, untamed waves. When she looked at me with those emerald green eyes, I was mesmerized by their warmth. "She was beautiful, and her nervous rambling only added to her charm."

"Poor thing. She escaped a terrible date, only to be stuck with your cranky behind."

"You do know you're supposed to be nice to me, right?" I tease.

The distant sound of running water and the clink of glasses comes through the phone. Martha is likely multitasking and washing the dishes while we talk. She doesn't like to stay still while she's on the phone.

"I don't sugarcoat the truth, honey. You can be a handful, even on your best days." She laughs, seemingly entertained by her own words.

"Glad I amuse you," I deadpan.

"Does this mystery woman have a name?" Martha asks, ignoring my sarcastic tone.

I consider not telling her, but I can already predict how that would go.

"Reese," I say hesitantly. "She left the tattoo shop without giving me any other information, and three months later, I found out she'd recently started working at Thompson & Tate. Honestly, I never thought I'd see her again."

"You like this girl, don't you?" Martha's voice raises an

octave. "Oh, Dawson, that's wonderful." I can almost hear her bouncing with enthusiasm.

Is it that obvious?

"Whoa, slow down." I rake my fingers through my hair, trying to calm my nerves. "Who said I like her?"

Martha scoffs, and the sound of running water abruptly stops. "You didn't have to; your voice says it all."

When I first went to live with the Tates, I was skeptical of their motives. It was summer, and I stayed holed up in my room, waiting for them to send me back. Every afternoon, Martha brought me a ham and cheese sandwich because the social worker told her they were my favorite. After seeing the sketchpad overflowing with designs I took everywhere, she got me a new one and a collection of pens. She was in tune with my emotions, anticipating what I needed before I did, and that's never changed.

"Why don't you tell me more about Reese?" she prompts.

I sit in my office chair, propping my feet up on the desk. "She's studying for the LSAT and plans to go to law school. Unlike me, she has no interest in corporate law. She wants to have a career advocating for kids."

"Like Colby," Martha says fondly. "She sounds like a wonderful person."

A soft smile plays on my lips. "She is," I agree.

Far better than I deserve.

"Have you told her about your past?" Martha broaches the subject carefully.

"She knows the basics."

Martha sighs her relief. "That makes me very happy to hear. I know how difficult it is for you to open up and share parts of yourself with others."

Usually, it's a challenge. I even struggle with sharing certain things with Colby and her, especially about my past, even though they've known me since I was fifteen. But with Reese, it feels different. I want her to know more about me—the real me.

"Did you catch the part where I said I'm her boss?"

Martha huffs in irritation. "Dawson Cole Tate, you're a high-powered attorney in New York. I'm well aware of the intimidation tactics you use to get your way. So, I don't buy it for a second that you couldn't find a way around a non-fraternization policy if you wanted to."

"Reese is only twenty-three," I add.

"Are you trying to talk me or yourself out of liking this woman?" Martha retorts. "Sometimes the heart defies all logic. You might not want to listen or fully grasp what it's trying to tell you, but from experience, it's best to trust in the process." Her voice softens. "You deserve to be happy, Dawson. If there's a possibility you've found someone who brings out the best in you, don't let her slip between your fingers. There's no telling if you'll ever get a chance like it again—"Martha's voice fades, followed by the sound of a door opening and Colby's voice announcing that he's home.

"I'm putting you on speakerphone," Martha tells me.

"Okay."

"Hey, son. Everything okay?" Colby asks me. "It's not like you to call so late."

"That's what I said," Martha chimes in. "He needed some advice. He met a woman named Reese and really likes her," she whispers.

"You do know I can hear you, right?"

"I was just looping Colby in, that's all." Martha feigns innocence.

"All I can say, son, is that when it comes to matters of the heart, Martha knows best."

"Aww, thanks, love," Martha croons, followed by the distinct sound of a kiss.

I wrinkle my nose. I'll never get over their displays of affection. "Well then, I'll let you lovebirds go. Talk to you later."

"We love you," they say in unison.

"Love you too."

When I hang up, I walk over to the window. It's dark out, and the skyline is dotted with lights from the neighboring buildings and billboards in the distance.

I think about Colby and Martha's relationship, which is defined by enduring love and centered around prioritizing each other's happiness.

Tonight is the perfect example: after a long day, Colby came home to Martha and greeted her with a welcome home kiss and a listening ear. On days when Martha deals with a challenging client, Colby brings her flowers and arranges a spa day to help her unwind. They're mindful of how to brighten each other's day and provide constant comfort and support. Even after twenty years of marriage, they're more in love than ever, their affection growing with each passing year.

I've had the privilege of seeing firsthand what a healthy, long-term romantic relationship looks like. I've never entertained the thought of what it could be like to experience something similar, until recently.

Reese has changed everything.

If there's a possibility you've found someone who brings out the best in you, don't let her slip between your fingers.

Martha's words keep running through my head.

The only thing I know for sure is that my day improves exponentially when Reese is there. Even the smallest interactions have me in better spirits. When she's having a bad day or struggling with something, I want to be the one who makes things better. And the prospect of waiting until Monday to see her again is disconcerting.

After a quick search through the employee files, I find her

address and then head down to the parking garage to get my bike.

An hour later, I'm sitting across from Reese's house in Brentsville, a neighborhood in Brooklyn. From my understanding, she lives alone, and it's unsettling to think she calls this part of town home.

The outside of her place is rundown, with cracked bricks, crumbling front steps and a rusted gate that is barely hanging on. Nevertheless, the yard is freshly mowed, and the leaves from the maple tree in the corner have been raked into a neat pile. Even though it's well past midnight, the light in the living room is on.

As I stride up the driveway, the crisp autumn air cuts through my leather jacket, a reminder that fall is in full swing.

I rap on the door. "Reese, it's Dawson," I call out.

I hear shuffling footsteps and the faint click of a deadbolt being turned before the door cracks open and Reese peeks outside.

Her hair is piled loosely into a bun and she's not wearing a stitch of makeup, giving me an unobstructed view of the freckles scattered across the bridge of her nose.

Damn, she's beautiful.

Her eyebrows knit together when she sees me. "Dawson, what are you doing here?"

"Are you going to invite me in?"

Reese chews on the inside of her cheek and glances over her shoulder before turning her attention back to me. "Did I forget to take care of something before I left the office?" she asks, disregarding my question altogether.

I try to get a better glimpse inside, but she keeps the door slightly open, leaving only a narrow gap of light.

"After you left, it was impossible to focus on anything else. I didn't want to wait until Monday to see you again, not with how we left things."

Her expression softens and she gives me a small smile.

The distant sound of a honking horn has me glancing around, a reminder that she still hasn't invited me inside.

"Can I come in so we can talk?" I ask.

"Why don't we go somewhere?" Reese suggests. "I'll be right out."

Alarm bells go off in my head as she tries to close the door. I wedge my shoe in the gap to keep it open, making it clear we're not going anywhere until I find out the reason she doesn't want me to come inside.

"Red, please let me in," I urge her.

She eyes me warily, sighing in defeat. "Fine," she mutters. "But keep an open mind, okay?"

Reese's words don't reassure me, and when she finally opens the door, I step past her into the entryway, not willing to risk her changing her mind.

As soon as I cross the threshold, I'm met with a cold draft. The air is so frosty that I swear I can see my breath. That's when I see Reese bundled up in a hoodie, layered with a jacket, wearing fuzzy socks and fingerless gloves.

What the hell?

Before I can ask her about it, my eyes wander to the living room on the left, which appears to be in the middle of a remodel. One wall has a fresh coat of gray paint, complemented by a refurbished bookshelf in the corner and a well-worn loveseat. The other half of the room is covered in peeling wallpaper and cluttered with piles of construction materials and tools.

The place is a hazardous construction zone, not a suitable living environment.

My lips tighten into a thin line. "In the middle of a renovation?" I ask, glancing over at Reese.

She's standing in front of the closed door, her face a blank slate, intently watching my response to seeing her place. "Sorry, it's such a mess. I was going to wait to do this room until I could afford to paint the entire thing, but I found a gallon of gray paint on clearance at the hardware store last month and couldn't pass it up." There's a tick in my jaw when she rubs her hands together like she's trying to stay warm. "The sofa isn't anything special, but it belonged to my grandparents, and I picked up the bookshelf at a nearby yard sale…" She trails off when she notices my incredulous stare.

"Why is it so cold in here?" I decide to start with the most straightforward question.

Reese's cheeks flush and she tugs her jacket tighter, trying to shield herself from the biting cold.

"The furnace is out," she explains.

"Since when?"

She averts her gaze, as if wishing I would disappear.

"A while," she answers vaguely.

Goddammit. Guilt washes over me as I think about how she's been coming here every night while I've been enjoying the comfort of my brownstone in Brooklyn Heights, with heated floors and a fireplace for particularly cold nights.

She hugs herself tightly. "This is my childhood home." It makes me want to hold her in my arms, but I wait for her to finish her story. "My grandpa kept it in good shape, but after he passed away and Grams moved to an assisted living facility, I couldn't keep up with maintaining it. The furnace is just the latest repair, adding to the mounting list of issues I've been trying to manage."

I rake my fingers through my hair, forcing myself to remain calm. "What other issues?"

She lets out a humorless laugh. "You might want to grab a pen and paper. A pipe recently burst in the bathroom and I had to pay a fortune for an emergency plumber to fix it. The windows are drafty, which makes the already chilly conditions worse; the floorboards in the corner of my grandparents' old bedroom are rotting; and the spare room has a mold problem." My stomach drops at the mention of mold while she ticks the problems off on her fingers. "Oh, and I'm pretty sure there's a mouse living in the kitchen wall because there are small holes and signs of gnawing around the kitchen cabinets." It makes sense now why she's been working two jobs. We pay well at Thompson & Tate, but it sounds like it's not enough to cover all her expenses, including unexpected costs like plumbing repairs.

It's partly my fault for not pressing her harder for answers. I let my attraction to her take precedence, making me blind to her struggles. Now, I have to find a way to set things right while being careful not to scare her off in the process.

If I were in her position, Martha and Colby would be here, taking care of the repairs and restoring the place to livable conditions without even being asked.

Reese doesn't have anyone other than her Grams.

At least not that she's mentioned. I know her grandpa is gone, her mom passed when was little, and she never knew her dad.

"Does Noah know about your living conditions?" I ask.

She stiffens, her posture rigid. "No, I haven't told him," she admits. "We usually study at his house or meet up at the library. I've never invited him over."

It feels like the wind has been knocked out of me when the realization that she really has been dealing with this all on her own sets in. She's putting on a brave face, pretending it doesn't bother her that the home she grew up in is in shambles, but I can see the strain behind her forced smile and the pains she's trying to conceal.

I can't stand the distance any longer. I step forward with my arms open. I'm relieved when she doesn't hesitate, stepping into my embrace like it's where she belongs.

"I'll pay to replace the furnace." It's a practical solution. I can afford it, and she shouldn't have to worry about something so basic when she has so much else going on.

Reese lifts her head, narrowing her eyes. "I'm not letting you do that." Determination hardens her expression. "I don't want your charity. I've managed perfectly well on my own. Truly, I appreciate the offer, but I can't accept it."

I hold her tighter, afraid she'll slip through my fingers if I let go. I'm used to steamrolling over obstacles in my way, but I'm learning with Reese that patience is key. That doesn't mean I won't take advantage of any loopholes if they present themselves.

"I'm willing to compromise," I concede, but her sidelong glance tells me she's not convinced. "You've got two choices: either come to my place, or I'll get you a hotel room." I shake my head when she tries to object. "Staying here tonight isn't an option. This place is an icebox, and you don't have any way to keep warm. And no, a jacket and some fuzzy socks don't cut it."

She grunts in irritation but doesn't pull away. "I've managed without a furnace for almost two months," she says, though her shivering makes her argument less believable.

I brush a loose lock of hair away from her face and lean in to press my forehead against hers. "Please do this for my peace of mind." My tone is almost pleading as I gaze into her emerald eyes. "You're not in this alone, Red. Not anymore."

She releases a shuddered breath, her eyes softening as she

leans into my touch. "I'll stay at your place, but only for one night. Tomorrow I'll figure something else out."

I relax my shoulders and take a deep breath, grateful she chose the first option. I'm not ready to say goodbye to her tonight.

There's no chance I'm letting her come back here in this condition, but that's a discussion for another time. This place holds sentimental value for Reese, and she'd never forgive me if I tried to have it condemned or renovated without her consent. For now, I need to make sure she's safe and comfortable, and that means getting her out of here.

I press a kiss to her forehead. "Do you have a backpack?"

She nods. "Yeah, why?"

"Go pack it, and we'll head out."

She gives me a wary glance as she steps away.

Ten minutes later, she comes out of her bedroom with a black backpack slung over her shoulder, her hair down, framing her face. She's in jeans, a hoodie, and hot pink sneakers with hand-drawn orchids on the sides. with a black backpack slung over her shoulder.

"Ready to go?" I ask.

The sooner we get out of this hazard zone, the better.

"Yeah," Reese says, a small shiver running through her.

I usher her out of the house as quickly as possible. She locks up and follows me into the street, pausing when she sees my bike.

Her mouth drops open. "*You* ride a motorcycle?"

A playful grin tugs at my lips. "Yeah, I do."

"Guess that explains why you asked me to bring the backpack," she says, motioning to her shoulder.

I take the helmet from the lock box and put it on Reese's head, gently tugging the straps to make sure it's secure.

"Where's your helmet?" she asks.

"I only have one, and your safety is the most important." I trail my fingers across her cheek, feeling the warmth of her skin against mine. She leans into my touch, and for a heartbeat, the world fades away as she gazes up at me with eyes that reflect the longing in mine. Reluctantly, I pull back, struggling to mask the urge to keep her close and never let go.

I clear my throat. "It's late. We better get going," I say as I swing my leg over my bike. "Hop on."

My night just took an unexpected turn, and I can't shake the feeling that tonight might change everything between Reese and me.

CHAPTER 14

Reese

I CLIMB ONTO THE BACK OF DAWSON'S BIKE AND SLIDE MY arms around his torso. I'm caught in a haze of disbelief. Leaving the office earlier, I came to terms with the possibility that I'd never have the chance to be this close to him again. Now, here I am, riding to his house on the back of his motorcycle, excited to see where the night takes us.

"You ready?" Dawson asks, his voice cutting through the hum of the engine.

"All set," I say, unable to meet his eyes through the helmet's visor.

He pulls onto the street and the engine's purr resonates through me. The wind whips around us as he speeds up, the city lights reflecting off the road ahead. With every turn, I lean closer to press my body against his and rest my head against his shoulder blades.

When we approach a stoplight, a group of women in clubbing attire catch sight of Dawson from their spot on the sidewalk.

They giggle and toss flirtatious glances his way, with one of them giving him a sultry wink.

I cast them a glare, even though the helmet conceals my expression. As they keep their collective gazes fixed on Dawson, I trail my fingers down his torso, his body tensing beneath my touch, and he grips my hand in his, kissing my palm.

The last thing I see before we speed off is the women's playful smiles turn to envious stares as they watch us ride away.

By the time we arrive at his picturesque brownstone in Brooklyn Heights, the tension between us is palpable. With every brush of his body against mine, my desire for him grows.

The exterior of his house is white sandstone, accented with black window frames, railings, and an imposing double-paneled front door. A maple tree nearby has vibrant red and orange leaves, adding a splash of autumn color to the urban landscape.

Dawson eases the bike into the ground-floor garage, and I keep my arms around him until he cuts the engine. When he glances back, I'm surprised to find he has a grin on his face.

"I like having you on the back of my bike," he states.

While this carefree version of him is unexpected, I enjoy it.

I take off my helmet, holding it in one hand. "I like the view from here," I whisper, my breath tickling his ear. "Especially with you in control."

"Keep that up, and we'll never make it inside," he says as he dismounts and helps me off the bike.

As much as I wouldn't mind him making good on that promise, I'm curious to see his place.

He takes my backpack and slings it over his shoulder. I follow him into the house, and he leads me into a stunning foyer. The place looks like it's straight out of a design magazine. Every piece of furniture looks handpicked to complement the gas-burning fireplace and the original crown molding—from the white chesterfield sofa to the gray armchairs with golden metal arm-rests, and the low-profile coffee table.

Dawson doesn't strike me as someone who cares about how the furniture or decor looks, but whoever designed the space has a talent for creating a stylish yet inviting atmosphere.

"Who would have guessed you're a fan of throw pillows," I tease, motioning to the white tasseled pillows on the couch.

"That was Martha's doing." Dawson chuckles as he sets my backpack on the couch. "She decorated the place."

My eyes widen at the mention of another woman. "Who's Martha?" I ask, more curious than anything.

"She is my... She and her husband, Colby, adopted me when I was sixteen." There's pride in his voice when he speaks about them.

I don't push him for further details, trusting that he'll tell me more when he's ready.

"She did an amazing job." My eyes drift to the floor-to-ceiling windows that offer a panoramic view of the Manhattan skyline. Moonlight streams through the glass, bathing the foyer in a soft, natural glow. "This place is incredible."

"I'm glad you like it." His gaze is heated, tracking my every move.

I tilt my head. "Why are you giving me that look?"

"What look?" he asks, with a straight face.

"The one that reminds me of an antihero in a romance novel who's plotting to lock me away in a tower until I fall for him." My voice drops to a playful whisper as I walk toward him.

My pulse picks up when he gives me a teasing smirk and adjusts his cufflinks. "This house might not have a tower, but I do have a wine cellar that might do the trick."

"If you leave me alone with your wine, I might drink the most expensive bottle in protest, and I'm a terrible drunk." I reach out, my hand drifting across his chest to smooth away a nonexistent wrinkle.

"Don't worry, if you ended up drinking too much, I'd keep you out of trouble." His voice is low and husky.

"What if I'm looking for a little trouble?" I let my fingers trace a slow path down the fabric of his shirt, in teasing strokes, hovering near his belt, fueling the charged energy between us. Dawson has a way of making me act boldly and I'm inclined not to hold back any longer.

He catches my hand, his grip gentle but firm, and murmurs, "Careful what you wish for, Red."

I swallow hard. "Isn't this the part of the night when you're supposed to show me the guest room, and we go our separate ways?" I ask, taunting him.

Please say no.

"If that's what you want." His voice is unreadable, but his eyes betray the restraint he's barely holding on to.

"And if I prefer another option?"

"Which is?"

"For you to take me to your room and spend the night showing me what I've been missing." I close the gap between us, my chest pressing against his, and exhale before asking, "Do you want me, Dawson?"

He cradles my jaw in his hand and holds my gaze, his eyes fixated on mine. "I've wanted you since the night you stepped into the tattoo shop." His voice drops low. "And right now, there's nothing I want more than to take you up to my bedroom, strip you bare, and take my time worshiping every single inch of your delectable body." His stubble brushes against my cheek. "But it has to be your decision."

"What if I only want one night? No strings attached?"

For now, I just want to live in the moment without thinking

about the consequences of our decisions or what tomorrow might bring.

"Then I'll have to give you a reason to stay longer because one night isn't enough time to do all the wicked things I have planned," Dawson promises.

I square my shoulders as I let out a shuddered exhale. "Take me to bed, Mr. Tate," I state, making my intentions clear.

A broad grin lights up Dawson's face. "I thought you'd never ask Ms. Taylor." He lifts me into his arms, and my legs lock around his waist.

Our bodies brush together, creating an intoxicating friction, with one hand clutching his neck to hold myself in place and the other trailing along the collar of his dress shirt. His heady scent fills the air, and I tilt my head forward, licking along the corded muscle of his neck unable to resist. He tightens his grip on my hips, grunting when my tongue grazes his jawline.

Once we make it to his bedroom on the second floor, Dawson sets me down, my hardened nipples rubbing against his chest as I glide down his body. My gaze moves to the bulge in his pants, and my fingers trace over the outline of his impressive erection.

He places his hand over mine, his expression tight. "Let's get you out of these clothes." He motions to my outfit. "Lift your arms," he orders.

I do as he says and he tugs my hoodie over my head, discarding it on the ground. His hot breath tickles my skin as he peppers kisses along my neck. He unclasps my bra, releasing my aching breasts from their confines, and his pupils flare as he grazes my nipples in teasing strokes. I whimper when he rolls them between his fingers, pinching them roughly.

We've only just begun and I'm already consumed by need. If foreplay with Dawson Tate feels this good, I'm anxious to experience what sex with him is like.

"God, I love that you're so responsive," he says, his voice deep and husky.

I gasp in protest when he releases my nipples, a flash of pain rippling through me.

He unbuttons my jeans and tugs them down my legs along with my underwear. I step out of them and push them to the side with my foot.

Dawson grips my chin, crushing his lips to mine in a searing kiss that leaves me breathless. "You're so fucking sexy," he rasps against my mouth. "Hold on tight," he urges, lifting me back into his arms. I put my hands on his shoulders as he carries me to the bed. He gently lies me in the middle of the mattress, leaning forward to press a kiss to my forehead.

He stands beside me fully clothed, while my body is laid out on display for him—proof that he's in control tonight. The contrast fuels the red-hot arousal racing through me, and I have the sudden urge to hear him call me his good girl again.

Dawson kneels on the bed and leans down to brush his hands up my legs, leaving a trail of goosebumps in his wake. I wait with bated breath as he plants a kiss on my knee. His stubble rubs against my skin as he moves up my thigh inch by torturous inch. My legs quake with anticipation when he reaches my apex.

He slowly licks along the seam of my pussy before plunging his tongue inside. I buck my hips, grinding against his face as I grip his hair with my fists. He eagerly explores, alternating between licking and sucking. When he thrusts two thick fingers inside me, a shiver courses through my veins.

I gasp at the heat rippling through my core. "Fuck, Dawson." I lift my hooded gaze to meet his heated stare.

"Damn, you're fucking drenched, Red."

I whimper, unable to find my voice, when he inserts a third finger, pumping in and out of me in a steady rhythm while massaging my clit in languid circles. My body coils tighter with each thrust, a wave of euphoria washing over me. I beg him with my eyes, a silent plea to pick up the pace.

"Come for me, angel."

I cry out when Dawson pinches my clit between his fingers, commanding my release, and I fall apart at his touch. My head drops back against the mattress as I call out his name savoring every delicious sensation.

"I can't wait another second to be inside you," he rasps. "Please tell me you haven't changed your mind."

"Never."

He gets off the bed and strips out of his clothes, leaving them in a pile on the floor. I run my tongue across my lips, my eyes locked on Dawson. It's the first time seeing him naked, his tattoos on full display. The ink on his skin is like a tapestry telling the story of who he is through bold artwork.

When he gets back on the bed, he hovers over me, silent as I explore; my fingers trail across a maze of roses with thorns winding around his right forearm, seamlessly blending in with the tail of a phoenix rising from the flames, its wings outstretched and the head resting on his shoulder.

"These are so beautiful, Dawson," I murmur.

He lets out a shuddered breath when my fingers glide to the center of his chest where there's a majestic lion's head with a flowing mane. Moving to his left upper arm, my touch navigates an elaborate geometric design, shifting from intricate details to abstract shapes that lead into the scales of justice below.

My hand finally hovers over a compass on his lower forearm that was the first piece to capture my attention.

My gaze drifts to the contours of his sculpted stomach, and I lick my lips with anticipation.

"You've got to be kidding me." I sigh dramatically, gesturing to his bare chest.

"What?" Dawson frowns, glancing down at himself.

"It's so unfair. You're thirty-five, and despite working around the clock, you still look like you belong on the cover of a romance novel."

He gives me a pointed look. "Are you suggesting I'm past my prime?"

"Never." I smirk.

"Why don't we put it to the test?"

I'm looking forward to it.

He reaches over to the nightstand to grab a condom, ripping open the package with his teeth. Once it's on, he grabs hold of his shaft and lines himself up with my entrance, running the tip of his dick along my seam in teasing strokes.

He kisses my forehead. "How are you doing, Red?" He restrains himself, a bead of sweat trickling down his forehead as he waits for my answer.

"I want you. Now," I beg.

"Damn you're sexy when you're bossy."

With one deep thrust, he pushes into the hilt. I gasp, relishing every glorious inch of him as he begins moving in earnest.

I wind my hands into his hair and tug him closer, molding my mouth to his. He grasps my jaw in his hand in response, deepening our kiss. Time seems to stand still as we're wrapped in our private haven where there are no expectations, requirements, or worries. Just two people driven by an unspoken longing, finally giving in to the blissful escape from reality.

"You're taking me so well, Reese," he rasps. "I can feel you clenching around my cock."

I can only whimper in reply, digging my heels into the mattress. He brushes his tongue against my lips before slipping it inside my mouth. I moan loudly as he picks up his pace, shifting the angle of his cock, pressing against my G-spot, and I gasp at the new sensation.

"I'm so close," I murmur.

I whine with disappointment when he slows his movements, pushing into me in short, shallow strokes, and I don't miss his smug smile as I squirm against him, desperate for release.

"What are you doing?" I protest.

"Savoring the moment, angel."

Our eyes lock, and I'm immersed in the feel of his sweat-slicked skin pressed against mine. His uneven breaths grazes my cheek, and the sensation of him pulsing inside me causes goosebumps to dance across my skin.

"Show me how you touch yourself, Red," Dawson murmurs.

My eyes remain on him as I reach between my legs, strumming my clit as his thrusts grow faster. When Dawson whispers, "Be my good girl and come all over my cock," my impending orgasm crashes over me.

I unravel beneath him, his roar of triumph filling the room as he finishes alongside me. He gently strokes my hair as we come down from our heightened pleasure.

"Are you okay?" he asks.

"Never been better," I assure him with a sated smile.

"Why don't we take a shower, and then I'll grab us something to eat."

"That sounds nice," I say drowsily. "I'm starving."

He scoops me into his arms, and I rest my cheek against his chest as he carries me to the bathroom. I haven't felt this content in a long time, and I wish this night would never end.

I wake to the faint scent of leather and sandalwood.

The first rays of sunlight filter through the window, signaling morning has arrived. I stifle a groan as I stretch—my entire body deliciously sore.

Dawson and I had sex in the shower last night—twice. He wrapped me in a plush towel and carried me to the bedroom, which led to him fucking me from behind on his already tousled sheets. His hand gripped firmly in my hair and my head arched back to face him as he drove into me, leaving imprints of his teeth on my neck and shoulder.

When we both finally collapsed from exhaustion, he drew me to his side and I fell asleep wrapped in his arms. One night with Dawson and I'm afraid I'm hooked. He makes me feel cherished in a way I never thought possible, and I find myself wanting to stay wrapped in his embrace forever.

As much as I wish that were a possibility, this magical moment will eventually come to an end, and we'll have to face reality.

For now, I set aside my nagging thoughts and concentrate on the present. As I roll over to greet Dawson, I'm caught off guard when I find his side of the mattress empty.

I scramble out of bed, clutching the sheet around me like a makeshift robe. After checking the bathroom and closet I go downstairs, each step echoing my mounting anxiety. A wave of disappointment washes over me when I get to the kitchen to find he's not there either.

Now that I think about it, he did agree to *just one night*. Maybe he's hoping I'll see myself out so he can avoid an uncomfortable morning-after conversation.

"Looking for me?" I spin around when I hear his deep timbre.

He's dressed in jeans, a white T-shirt, and a black biker jacket. It's the first time I've seen him out of his usual business attire, and he looks incredibly enticing.

"Good morning, beautiful." He sets a carafe of coffee and a brown paper bag onto the kitchen island. Striding over to me, he cups my face in his hands and presses a heated kiss to my lips. "Sorry I wasn't here when you woke up. I realized my fridge was empty and wanted to make sure you had breakfast." He pulls out a barstool at the kitchen island for me. "Take a seat and we'll eat."

My heart races at his kind gesture. "Thank you."

He hands me a warm sausage, egg, and cheese croissant and a cup of coffee. "It's a pumpkin spice latte. Your favorite."

The thought of this man remembering one of my favorite things makes my heart skip a beat.

"Thank you." I take a long sip, savoring the taste of cinnamon, nutmeg, and the creamy pumpkin that blends perfectly with the rich coffee. "It's so good."

He chuckles. "I'm glad you like it, but I still don't understand the hype. Pumpkin belongs in a pie, not a drink."

"You don't know what you're missing out on." I say, taking another drink. "If it wasn't seasonal I'd drink them all year-round."

A brief flicker crosses his face before he takes the seat next to me and unwraps his breakfast sandwich. "Now that we're both well rested, can we talk about why you're living in a house that's practically falling apart and feels like you're in the Arctic tundra?" he asks, his voice edged with worry.

I groan, wiping my hand across my face. As much as I'd rather sidestep this topic, Dawson's concern tells me he's not going to brush it off. Even though I might sound ungrateful, I do appreciate that he cares enough to ask.

"My grandpa bought the house as a wedding gift for my grandma. It started as a fixer-upper,
but with their teachers' salaries, money was tight and they couldn't afford to fully remodel it." I pause briefly, tucking a piece of hair behind my ear. "When life threw them curveballs, they decided to put their energy into keeping the place well-maintained. They lived there until my grandpa passed away a few years ago, and Grams moved into Oak Ridge shortly after."

Dawson glances down, adjusting the lid of his coffee cup.

"Do you mind me asking what happened to your parents? You haven't mentioned them."

Nothing gets past him. I rarely talk about my unconventional upbringing because people usually react awkwardly when they hear the details.

Dawson is the exception. Our backgrounds may be different—he grew up in foster care while my grandparents raised me—but we both know what it's like to grow up without our parents and the void that leaves behind.

"My mom got pregnant with me during college and never told us who my father was." I avert my gaze, not wanting to see Dawson's reaction to the next part. "She was diagnosed with stage four Hodgkin's lymphoma when I was a toddler and passed away not long after."

I'm forced to look up when Dawson puts his hand over mine, giving it a comforting squeeze. "I'm sorry you had to go through that, angel."

I let out a deep breath, glancing down at my hands. "It was a long time ago, and I was so young that my memories of her are fuzzy. There will always be a part of me that's missing, not having gotten the opportunity to grow up with my mom, but I was lucky to have my grandparents." I take a sip of my coffee, savoring the comforting taste of pumpkin spice. "They gave me the best childhood anyone could have asked for. That's why I want to pursue a career in law—to advocate for kids who don't have the same safety net or resources that I was fortunate to have."

"You have a beautiful soul, Reese Taylor." Dawson presses a kiss to the back of my hand, making my cheeks flush. "It wasn't until I was a teenager that I had someone willing to advocate for me, and not every kid gets that opportunity."

"It seems like we both dealt with less-than-ideal circumstances, but we made it out okay," I say, with a faint smile.

"Yeah, we sure did," he says, his eyes crinkling with warmth.

Dawson's childhood was undoubtedly harder than mine. I can't imagine the lack of stability from being moved around constantly without family to lean on.

The mood lightens as we both dig into our breakfast. I could so easily get used to lazy weekend mornings with Dawson, who makes me feel at ease and provides a sense of calm when the outside world is so chaotic.

When I grab a napkin from the counter to wipe my face, I notice him staring off into the distance, lost in thought.

"What's on your mind?"

He looks at me with a glint in his eye. "Spend the rest of the weekend with me," he says, like it's the simplest request in the world.

A flush creeps up my neck as I stare at him slacked jawed.

"You want me to stay with you for the weekend?" I ask, unsure if I heard him correctly.

He nods. "Yes, I do."

"I'm supposed to visit my grandma this afternoon," I say.

No matter how much I like spending time with him, I can't forget about my other responsibilities.

"I want to take you to the tattoo shop. There are some people I'd like you to meet. We'll be done in plenty of time for you to visit your grandma, then we can go out to dinner."

I'm intrigued by the prospect of visiting Steel & Ink again. I haven't been back since the night we met, and I'd love to see him in his element while he's tattooing. That side of his life is kept under lock and key, and he's showing me a great deal of trust by letting me in.

"I'd really like to visit the shop," I say.

"Great, it's settled then. We'll make a day of it." He gets up to toss his wrapper in the trash and heads toward the door.

"Dawson, wait," I call out.

He turns around to face me. "Yeah?"

"I work at the club tonight, and I can't afford to miss a shift," I explain.

He scratches the light stubble on his jaw as he studies me, his expression contemplative. "Would it help if I told you I'm giving you a bonus? Enough that you shouldn't have to work at the club anymore."

I'm out of my chair in record time. "No way. I'm not accepting special treatment." My voice betrays my anxiety as I nibble on my lower lip.

This is exactly what I wanted to prevent. If word got out, it could raise suspicions with HR and my coworkers, especially since I've only been there a short time, and it's unusual for new hires to receive bonuses.

He strides over to me, drawing me in for a hug. "Don't worry, Red. I'm giving one to each of the paralegals. You've all been working so hard, and it should be recognized."

I blink up at him, stunned. "That's very generous of you, but I haven't earned it. Everyone else should get it, but I'd rather it only goes to those who deserve it."

Dawson tilts my chin, pressing a kiss to my forehead. "Please let me take care of this… of you." he implores.

I swallow hard. "I'm not sure I can accept it."

"You're just as deserving as anyone else," he states.

I close my eyes, allowing myself to relax in his arms.

For so long, it's been me against the world. I've let my pride get in the way of asking for help. It's led me to place unrealistic expectations on myself, believing I had to be everything for everyone I love.

Since Dawson came into my life, he's upended my old way of thinking. He's shown me that leaning on someone doesn't make me weak—it means I'm strong enough to accept help when I need it most.

"Just this once, angel," Dawson says softly when I don't answer. "Please."

I open my eyes and am met with his warm, reassuring gaze.

"Okay… but only because you asked so nicely," I breathe.

I'll have to call David, my manager at the club, and let him know I won't be coming in tonight—or ever again.

There's no guarantee that it's the right decision, but I owe it to myself to take the risk. The extra time will allow me to study more and bring me one step closer to achieving my goal of becoming a lawyer.

CHAPTER 15

Dawson

WE ARRIVE AT THE SHOP, AND THE FAMILIAR SCENT OF ink and antiseptic fills the air.

Mickey is ringing up a customer and they wave goodbye as they exit. "Hey, boss, how's it going?" He glances at his watch. "You're here early today."

"Seren's coming in."

Seren is Christian's mom, and today we're finishing up the shading on her forearm sleeve. She's a nurse, so I've had to find time to get this done that works around her schedule.

Mickey nods knowingly, and a smile lights up his face when he notices Reese. "Who's this lovely lady?"

She offers him her hand. "I'm Reese. It's a pleasure to meet you."

"Likewise. I'm Mickey."

He gives me a sideways glance as he introduces himself. I don't share much about my personal life, and aside from Martha and Seren, I've never brought a woman to the shop.

"Come on, Red." I nod toward my workstation. "I've got to start prep."

My station is neat and organized, with a cabinet positioned against the wall that stores all of my supplies, a stool for me to work on, and a leather chair that reclines.

I set up two additional folding chairs while Reese walks around the outer perimeter, admiring the sample art on the walls. While I have a selection of flash designs available, I prefer to sketch custom designs for my clients. Many of them view tattoos as a form of catharsis and a way to heal from a traumatic experience. Creating something that holds special meaning is oftentimes part of that process.

"You have a gift," Reese says over her shoulder.

"So do you." I motion to her white sneakers decorated with sunflowers. "I've noticed you have quite the collection."

A blush spreads across her cheeks. "In seventh grade, my grandpa took me shoe shopping, and I saw a pair of expensive sneakers with a floral print that I liked. When he found a pair of discounted white ones in my size, he suggested we draw our own designs on them. He said I'd be the coolest kid in school for having a custom pair of sneakers." She glances down at the pair she's wearing. "I've been adding floral designs to my sneakers ever since.

"You're a natural, Reese. The flowers are incredible." I take out the tattoo machine, ink, and a few additional supplies I need for my appointment, arranging them on the tray I've set up on the counter.

Reese blushes. "Thank you. What about you? How did you discover your passion for drawing?"

"Growing up in foster care had its challenges, but drawing was my escape. My sketchbook became my voice, a place where I could express the things I couldn't say out loud." I sit on my stool, inserting a new needle into the tattoo machine. "As a teenager, I got into some trouble. There were occasions I wasn't permitted to draw, and it felt like losing a part of myself." I swallow hard as I push aside the painful memories.

"Have you ever been in prison?" Reese blurts out.

I can't help but burst out laughing. "Isn't that a question you should have asked before you slept with me?" I playfully tease.

After all these years, I can't believe that rumor is still making the rounds.

"Well?" she demands.

"No, Red, I've never been to prison. I did a few stints in juvie, though. The first time I was wrongly accused of stealing, but I was guilty for the rest. Colby was my public defender for the last case and was one of the few people who saw a side of me that wasn't my rap sheet."

Reese saunters toward me, stepping in between my legs. She winds her hands around my neck, her fingers weaving into my hair. "Why does the fact that you were a rebel make you that much sexier?"

I gaze up at her, a smirk playing on my lips. "I prefer the term misunderstood artist. When we get back to my place, I'll have to show you how rebellious I still am." I wrap my arm around her waist, cupping her ass, reveling in the small squeal that escapes her lips when I tug her closer. "Any more questions?"

"Did you ever consider becoming a tattoo artist full-time? Before you were a lawyer?"

I shake my head. "I didn't start tattooing until after law school, and I don't charge my tattoo clients for their ink."

"You don't charge them?" Reese sounds surprised.

"No. Most of them have scars they want to conceal and are looking to cover up painful memories. Or are ex-convicts wanting a symbol of redemption. It's rewarding to help others reclaim their power and help them heal from their past experiences."

For me tattooing is a way to give back to the community and

create a positive change in people's lives who otherwise might not have an outlet for self-expression.

Before Reese can respond, the sound of approaching footsteps has her moving my hands from her ass and taking a step back. I look up just in time to see Christian running into my station.

"Hey, Dawson." He throws his arms around me.

"Good to see you, kid," I say, ruffling his hair.

"Christian, honey, give Dawson some space," Seren says as she steps inside. "It's good to see you, Dawson." Seren gives me a grateful smile. "Thanks for giving Christian those Mavericks tickets, that was very generous of you."

"Of course."

Reese is standing in the corner of the station, watching our interaction with curiosity. She isn't accustomed to seeing me interact with the people I'm closest to. She's only seen me in the office where I'm gruff and demanding with my employees.

"This is Reese." I tell Christian and Seren.

"It's nice to meet you," Seren says, giving her a wave.

"Christian, why don't you take a seat over there while I work on your mom's tattoo?" I gesture to one of the folding chairs I set up earlier.

"I'll hang with you if that's okay." Reese smiles.

Christian shrugs. "Sure."

While they get settled, Seren slips off her jacket and hangs it on the rack in the corner. She's wearing a black tank top underneath, leaving her arm exposed for easy access. Her tattoo spans from her left wrist to her forearm—delicate vines and blooming flowers wrapped around a broken chain. During our last session I added mid-tones to bring the flowers to life, so all there's left to do is the shading.

Before getting started, I wash my hands, put on disposable gloves, and settle in my seat. As I examine the tattoo, I map out the final additions to incorporate a dimensional effect. I switch on the tattoo machine, steadying my hand with the familiar weight of the vibration against my palm.

Seren rests her head against the chair when I start, her eyes falling shut. She's told me that she finds this process therapeutic—the hum of the needle turns a painful memory into a beautiful and empowering symbol of resilience. After all she's sacrificed, I'm glad she's doing this for herself.

Halfway through I pause, standing to stretch out my neck and roll out my shoulders. I glance over to see Reese on the other side of the station with my sketchpad in her lap. Her lip is tucked between her teeth as she sketches what appears to be an orchid. Christian leans over her shoulder, captivated by the strokes of her pencil as each line brings the flower to life. Like me, Reese uses her art as a way to find peace amidst the chaos, letting her creativity guide her to a calmer place.

Seren opens her eyes, her gaze darting between Reese and me. "She's really pretty," Seren whispers so only I can hear. "I'm glad you've found someone. You deserve to be happy."

"Thanks." I give her a tight smile, deciding not to tell her that Reese isn't mine. Though the more time we spend together, the more I wish she were.

I turn my attention back to finishing Seren's tattoo, the alternative soundtrack Mickey has on in the shop providing the only background noise. Once I'm done, I clean the inked skin, apply ointment, and carefully wrap it.

"All set," I announce.

"I can't thank you enough," Seren says, gazing down at her arm. "Are you sure I can't pay you?"

"Positive."

She gets out of her chair to grab her things. "Christian, you ready to go?"

He snaps his head up from watching Reese draw. "Guess

what. Reese says she'll draw me a design on those white sneakers Dawson got me last month, how cool is that?"

"That's so nice of you to offer," Seren says to Reese.

"I'm happy to do it," Reese assures her with a genuine smile.

It's heartwarming to watch her interact with some of the people who matter most to me. Her ease with the situation makes me grateful to have her here. Not everyone would be comfortable spending their afternoon with a teenager they didn't know while I tattooed his mom.

"Can I go say bye to Mickey?" Christian asks Seren. "He promised he'd give me a soda once we finished."

"Sure. I'll go with you." She tucks her coat under her arm. "Thanks again, Dawson, and it was so good to meet you, Reese."

"You too." Reese waves goodbye as Seren slips out of my station.

Once they're out of view, Reece approaches. "Her tattoo is stunning," she murmurs. "I couldn't help but notice the scars. What happened to her?"

"Her ex-boyfriend used her as a human ashtray." I keep my voice lowered. "He's in prison now and will never hurt her or Christian again."

I've made sure of it.

A friend at the district attorney's office pressed charges a couple of years ago when damning evidence conveniently surfaced, linking Seren's ex to a drug trafficking ring.

"Christian and Seren are lucky to have you in their life." Reese chews her bottom lip, lost in thought. "Hey, Dawson?" she asks, placing her hand on my shoulder.

"Yeah?"

"Do you want to come with me to visit my grandma? Her name's Georgia." She holds her breath while waiting for me to reply.

I place my hand over hers. "Are you sure, Red? If you'd prefer to go alone, we can meet up for dinner after."

One way or another, we're spending the rest of the weekend together, but I'm not about to force her to introduce me to her grandma if she's not ready.

"Yes, I am," Reese states confidently. "Grams will be excited to meet you."

I arrive at Oak Ridge an hour later with a bouquet of red roses. Reese took a rideshare over earlier. Noah is the only guy she's introduced to her grandma so she wanted to tell her about me before I got here.

The receptionist at the front desk directs me to Georgia's room, and I knock softly when I get there.

"Come in," Reese calls out.

I open the door to find her sitting at her grandmother's side by the window.

"You must be Dawson." Georgia holds out her hand. "Reese, you didn't tell me he was so handsome."

Reese's cheeks flush. "Let's not inflate his ego any further."

Georgia's lips curve into a sly grin. "From the looks of him, it's not the only thing that's impossible to ignore, but you'd know best, now wouldn't you, sweetheart."

"Oh. My. *God*. Grams." Reese covers her mouth with her hand. "I cannot believe you just said that."

Georgia waves her off. "At my age, I've earned the right to speak my mind. There's nothing to be ashamed of."

I've only been here a minute, and I'm already a big fan of Reese's grandma.

I hold out the bouquet of roses for Georgia. "These are for you."

"Handsome *and* a gentleman." She grins, setting the flowers on the side table next to her.

I scan the room, taking in my surroundings. It's spacious, decorated with several personal touches, including a hand-stitched quilt on the bed, a curio cabinet displaying an array of tea sets, and a bureau lined with a collection of gold picture frames.

Several of the photos show Georgia and a man looking lovingly into each other's eyes, along with others that include Reese alongside them. On the far end, there is a photograph with a young woman who bears a striking resemblance to Reese. The woman is seated on the front porch of Reese's house. Her gaze, brimming with happiness, is directed at the baby she's cradling in her lap.

"That's Jodi, Reese's mom," Georgia says from her recliner, her voice taking on a wistful tone. "That picture was taken a week after she brought Reese home from the hospital. We were taken with her from day one."

I turn to Reese. "You look just like her," I observe.

She smiles. "Thank you."

"Not a day goes by that I don't think of Jodi," Georgia adds. "But when I look at my Reese, I see a piece of her mom and it brings me so much peace." She gives Reese a loving glance, her eyes glistening with unspoken memories.

"Love you, Grams," Reese says.

"Love you too, sweetheart." Georgia replies. She briefly glances at her watch, her expression changing to urgency. "We better get going or we'll be late."

"Where are we going exactly?" I ask.

Reese never mentioned a field trip.

"Oak Ridge has a weekly bingo night for residents and their families, and I never miss it," Georgia says enthusiastically.

"Tonight is special—I've never brought two guests before." She beams.

"Am I not good enough for you anymore?" Reese winks playfully.

"Oh honey, you're more than enough, but who could pass up the chance to bring along some eye candy. The other ladies will be talking about it for days."

"You hear that, Dawson? You're the *eye candy*," Reese taunts.

"Maybe my charm will throw them off their game and I'll win a round or two." I wink.

"Don't let Ms. Werther from across the hall hear you say that," Georgia warns me. "She considers herself the top contender for that title."

"I have to go grab something. I'll be right back." Reese gets out of her chair and disappears into the attached bedroom.

When she's out of earshot, I lean in closer to Georgia, resting my arm on her chair. "I want you to know I'm interested in your granddaughter," I explain in a whisper. "Have any advice for me?"

Georgia raises an eyebrow with a dry laugh. "What makes you think you're good enough for her? Your fancy job and deep pockets might impress some people, but not me, and most certainly not Reese."

It's clear that Reese is the most important person in Georgia's life, and I like that she doesn't sugarcoat her reservations in order to protect her granddaughter.

"There's no question Reese is too good for me" I openly admit. "But if I was lucky enough to call her mine someday, I'd make sure she was safe, happy and cherished"

Georgia gives me a skeptical look, like she's weighing whether to believe me or not. "If my husband were still here, he'd make sure you understood the repercussions of hurting Reese. As it stands, you'll have to deal with me," she states, her tone firm. "I may be an old lady, but don't underestimate me." Just when I think she's going to tell me to get lost she crooks her finger for me to come closer. "But if I were to offer a word of advice, I might recommend flowers. Reese is a romantic at heart and appreciates thoughtful gestures. Her grandfather used to bring us flowers every Friday and it was one of her favorite things."

Sending flowers to Reese's desk was a stroke of luck. Now that I know she likes mindful gestures, I'll have to find more ways to show her that I care.

Before I can respond to Georgia, Reese comes back into the living room, triumphantly holding up a canvas bag.

"I got the dabbers," she exclaims. "Ready to go?"

"The what?" If it wasn't already obvious that I've never played bingo before, it sure as hell is now.

"You'll see," Georgia says with a mischievous twinkle in her eye. "You're in for a fun evening."

Reese is sexy as hell with a neon orange dabber gripped tightly in her hand, a look of concentration on her face whenever the host hollers out a new number. Her eyes light up with excitement every time she's able to block out another square.

Georgia and Reese are serious about this game. Our table is lined with rows of dabbers they brought from Georgia's room. Each one has a unique pattern or image, from polka dots to cartoon faces, and some even have disco ball caps.

"BINGO," Reese shouts at the top of her lungs, waving her card in the air. She turns to Georgia with a grin. "I won again."

It's refreshing to see her so carefree. Georgia is her entire world and I'm grateful she allowed me a peek into this side of her life.

Georgia tilts her head with a subtle smirk. "You won't be so lucky during the next round, sweetheart," she teases. Several other residents cheer Reese on as she jogs up to the front of the room so the game host can examine her card.

"Is she always this competitive?"

"Absolutely. She got it from her grandfather. He made everything into a game when she was growing up." Georgia pushes aside her bingo card and takes a new one from the center of the table. "He passed away six years ago."

I place my hand over hers. "I'm sorry for your loss."

She pats my hand, giving me a soft smile. "I appreciate it. We were together for forty years, and it was an adjustment moving on without him." Her smile wavers. "During Reese's first semester of college, I slipped and fell, and she was ready to quit school to take care of me full time. I wasn't going to let that happen, so when a friend mentioned how great this facility was, I jumped at the chance to move here."

"I'm sure it was difficult for you to leave your house."

Georgia scoffs. "George did a wonderful job maintaining it while he was alive, but that place has always been a fixer-upper. I wish Reese would consider selling it. The property is worth more than the house, and she could put the money toward her education." She leans in closer and speaks in a whisper. "I'm not naive. She may not have told me, but it's obvious she's stretching herself thin. She's wanted to be a lawyer since she was a child, and I worry she might miss her chance."

I give Georgia's hand a gentle squeeze. "Mark my words, Reese will become a lawyer as long as that's what she wants."

I mean it. Even if she decides she no longer wants anything to do with me, I'll make sure has the resources to achieve her goals. After everything she's been through, she deserves to chase her dreams.

Georgia pats my cheek. "You're a good man, Dawson."

"Don't go around telling anyone, I have a reputation to uphold," I say with a playful grin.

Before she can respond, Reese comes back to our table with a soft blush-colored blanket. "Look what I won—" She holds it up triumphantly. "This is for you, Grams. I know you've been getting cold at night, so you can put this over your feet." She hands the blanket to Georgia. "It's not the cashmere one you've been wanting, but I hope it'll do for now."

"It's perfect, sweetheart. Thanks for thinking of me." Georgia presses a kiss to Reese's cheek.

Their interaction displays the genuine love they have for each other. Reese is attentive to even the smallest details and Georgia's love for her granddaughter goes beyond the norm.

It's clear that Reese has put aside her own needs to make sure her grandma is well taken care of and to keep the house where her grandparents lived their whole marriage. It makes me want to do whatever I can to lighten her load.

She'd never let me remodel her house, but there must be other ways I can help to make her life easier. As I glance around the room filled with Oak Ridge residents an idea begins to take shape. The more I think about it, the better it sounds. However, if I move forward, there are logistics that will need to be ironed out. In the meantime, I want to do something just for Reese this weekend. A chance to get away for a day without any responsibilities or interruptions, giving her a well-deserved break.

The bingo host instructs everyone to clear their boards so a new game can begin. Reese and Georgia get their dabbers ready, and I take it as my chance to make an important call.

"I'll be right back," I whisper to Reese.

"Sounds good," she says.

Once I'm in the hallway, I dial Harrison's number. It only rings twice before he picks up.

"This is Harrison," he answers coldly.

"I need to use my first favor," I state.

"Right now? I'm a little busy," Harrison grunts.

"It has to be done tomorrow," I say, glancing through the door at Reese, who's laughing at something Georgia said.

"Fuck, you're serious."

"You did tell me I could cash them in whenever I wanted," I remind him.

"Yeah, yeah, I know," he mutters. "My brothers and I will take care of it." I hear voices in the background.

"I'll text you the details." I hang up and shoot a quick text to the private jet charter I use.

With careful planning and Harrison's help, tomorrow will be perfect. Now I just have to break the news to Reese that she'll be spending the rest of the weekend with me and hope she agrees to go with me.

CHAPTER 16

Reese

AFTER BINGO, WE DECIDED TO HAVE DINNER WITH GRAMS before coming back to Dawson's place. I was pleasantly surprised at how quickly they hit it off. Dawson can be charismatic when he wants to be.

Usually, I'm in low spirits after a visit with Grams, the loneliness hitting hard after leaving her, but today was different. Dawson's company has kept the sadness at bay, and for that I'm grateful.

We step out onto the roof, where a pool is surrounded by three ivy-covered walls providing a secluded retreat and offering a stunning view of the waterfront. The patio is furnished with loungers and a table, a cushioned sofa, and two heated lamps that Dawson switches on as I take in the surroundings.

"This is amazing," I say, awestruck.

"You want to go for a swim?" Dawson asks, nodding toward the pool. "It's heated."

I look wistfully at the water. "I didn't pack a swimsuit," I remind him.

He failed to mention the hidden oasis on his rooftop beforehand.

"You don't need one," he says with a wry grin.

I watch him with a hint of skepticism as he proceeds to strip out of his long-sleeve shirt and pants, tossing his clothes on the nearby patio table. His boxers hang low on his hips, and his well-defined muscles and confident stance are on full display. He's devastatingly attractive, and it's almost criminal how he wields it.

The tattoo of the phoenix rising from the ashes on his right bicep catches my attention—its wings outstretched and the head splayed out on his shoulder. Now that he's shared more of his past, it makes sense why he got it—a symbol of beating the odds and overcoming early hardships to achieve success.

"Your turn." He nods toward my outfit.

He watches, his jaw slightly open as I unfasten the buttons of my pants and slowly tugs them down over my hips. Once they fall to the ground, I step out one leg at a time and kick them out of the way. I shoot him a sultry glance as I gradually lift my shirt over my head, and he groans. His patience wears thin when he catches his first glimpse of my bra, amplifying the thrill of the reaction I provoke in him.

Once I'm down to my bra and underwear, he closes the distance between us, takes me by the hand, and leads me to the pool steps. He was right. The pool is warm when we step in. The water envelops me and the slight chill in the air fades away.

I release Dawson's hand and wade farther into the pool. I lie back, stretch out my arms, and drift on the water's surface, feeling a sense of weightlessness. My legs extend, occasionally shifting with the gentle current. I allow myself to relax, my eyes fluttering shut, lost in the soothing rhythm of the water.

Floating in the pool brings a sense of relaxation I haven't felt in ages. Today was perfect and gave me a peek into who Dawson is outside of the office.

From a distance, he comes across as a hard-edged lawyer, but in truth, he's kind, generous, and surprisingly thoughtful. He's taken every opportunity to find ways to lighten my load and I'm left with a startling realization—I could be in danger of falling in love with Dawson Tate.

With every moment we share I see beyond his tailored suits and brash demeanor. My feelings are shifting into genuine affection, and I'm afraid it could turn into something so much more.

I have a complex history with love, marked by losing some of the people I cared about most.

But even though being with Dawson makes me giddy and has my heart racing when we're together, I can't forget that he's still my boss.

My eyes flutter open as the water ripples, finding him standing a few feet away, his gaze fixed on me. The weight of his stare holds me captive as I tread water, my feet unable to reach the bottom of the pool.

He swims toward me, my heart pounding so loudly I wonder if he can hear it. The space between us dwindles, and my racing thoughts dissipate. He has a gift for making me feel cherished and safe when we're together. As he draws me into his chest, I instinctively wrap my legs around him, wanting to stay anchored in his embrace.

His thumb gently traces the worry line etched in the crease of my brow. "Something on your mind?" he asks.

Despite my reservations, I choose to fully embrace this moment because there's no guarantee we'll have another like it.

"Why don't I show you instead?"

I slant my mouth across his, and my moan reverberates through our kiss as his tongue dances with mine, leaving me gasping for air. He moves toward the pool's edge, effectively pinning me against the wall, and nuzzles my neck, inhaling deeply as if memorizing my scent.

"You're perfect, Red," he murmurs.

His gaze locks on mine as he tugs down my panties, lifting one leg at a time to take them off. He tosses the wet underwear onto the pool deck before his focus returns to kissing me.

My hands move to his hair, sinking my nails into his scalp, drawing him closer. His fingers trail against my neck before disappearing into the water, grazing my breast, then my navel. He pauses when he gets to my core.

"I can't do what I want to you while we're in the water," he says.

His fingers imprint on my thighs as he carefully carries me out of the pool and moves across the patio to one of the loungers. He bends down to lay me on the cushion, stealing another kiss before pulling away with a smug smile.

A blush spreads across my cheeks as he brushes his hands along my legs, sending a tantalizing shiver down my spine. When he pulls my legs apart, Dawson lets out a guttural groan.

I wait with bated breath as he leans into the apex of my thighs, nipping at my sensitive skin. When I try to shift in my seat, he holds my legs apart, pressing his nose against my core and inhaling my scent. He doesn't hesitate to plunge his tongue inside my pussy, and my back arches off the lounger as I cling to the sides and buck my hips, grinding against his face.

God, why is that so hot?

A rush of heat courses through me as Dawson hikes my legs over his shoulders to get a better angle, and I wind my fingers in his hair to keep myself steady. He steals my breath when he circles my clit in an intoxicating rhythm.

"Don't stop, please don't stop," I moan.

"I'm going to worship your body until you're unable to walk straight," he vows before burying his face back between my thighs.

"Oh my god," I gasp out as I dig my nails deeper into his scalp.

"Damn, you taste so sweet," he utters.

I pant heavily as my climax builds, and my legs tighten around Dawson's head when he locks his mouth around my clit. As I cry out, begging for more, he bites down firmly, and the night air fills with my screams as I erupt, tumbling into orgasmic bliss.

"Fuck, you're sexy as hell when you come for me," Dawson groans.

When I finally drift back from my euphoric state, I lower my hooded eyes to meet his unwavering gaze.

Dawson pushes my hair from my face as he kisses along the bridge of my nose. "I'm not done with you yet. Not by a long shot."

A tingle of anticipation courses through my core as he reaches behind me to unfasten my wet bra, dropping it to the ground. He kisses the valley between my breasts next, and I draw in a sharp breath when he flicks one of my nipples with his tongue. The small bud hardens at his touch, and he greedily wraps his mouth around it, biting down on the soft flesh.

"Holy fuuu-"

"That's right, baby, let me make you feel good," he groans.

I sink my fingers back into his hair and tug. My moans grow louder as he alternates between licking, biting, and sucking my sensitive breasts. I cling to him, savoring the attention he's lavishing on me.

His hand trails down my chest until he gets to my stomach, drawing patterns with the pads of his fingers. When he reaches my legs, they fall open, eager to accept his touch. My breath hitches when he sinks two fingers inside me, stilling for a moment before starting to push in and out at a steady pace.

"*Dawson.*" I moan his name like a prayer, my back arching at the welcome intrusion.

He leans forward, not allowing a single inch of space between us, and runs his tongue across the column of my neck while kissing along my collarbone. My head falls back against the headrest. This man has me coming completely undone and I wouldn't stop it even if I could. A soft hum escapes my lips as I remember the feel of his thick cock inside me.

"You're so stunning, Reese, and when you're unraveling for me? There's nothing more beautiful" He sigh. "Fuck." He pulls away and runs his fingers through his hair. "I don't have a condom out here. I'll be right back." He moves to get up, but I grab his arm to stop him.

I've never had sex without protection before, yet the image of Dawson inside me without a barrier is exhilarating.

"I'm on birth control. We don't need a condom… unless you want one," I add.

"Are you sure?" His expression is serious. "I've never gone without one before and would never do anything to make you uncomfortable."

I draw him closer, kissing him on the lips. "Positive. Fuck me, Dawson. Fuck me right now."

"Gladly, Red."

He strips out of his sopping wet boxers and aligns himself with my core, pushing inside slowly. I slam my eyes shut and grip him tighter as our intermingled groans vibrate around us.

Once fully seated, he pauses to give me a moment to adjust. "Holy shit. You're so goddamn tight," he grits out, voice strained.

"God, I'll never get over how big you are," I gasp.

"Don't worry, angel, you can take me," he promises.

Dawson quivers beneath my touch from the strain of holding back. When he starts moving, I meet him thrust for thrust, embracing the sensation of him inside me. This man has me under his spell, and I'm powerless against his seductive touch.

"I'm so close, Dawson," I pant out.

"We're going to come together," he orders, pressing a kiss to my temple.

He picks up his pace and all rational thought is gone as the primal sound of flesh slapping against flesh resonates in the air. I dive into a state of euphoria and when I look up at him, he's watching me, silently promising to give me more.

"Come for me, angel," he rasps as he flicks my clit repeatedly, giving me the added friction I've been begging for. My mouth parts, and a shiver courses through my spine as I detonate like a bomb. He's right behind me, letting out a guttural groan as we tumble into a state of oblivion together.

Dawson cradles my face, planting soft kisses across my cheeks and forehead, leaving a trail of warmth behind.

He gently pulls out of me and retrieves his shirt from the table to clean us up. He tosses it to the ground and sits next to me on the lounger.

"How are you feeling?" he asks.

I give him a sated smile. "Couldn't be better. Although I'm not sure I'll be able to walk down the stairs." My body is boneless, and I'm achy in all the best ways.

Dawson gently caresses my cheek with his thumb. "Don't worry, I'll take care of you."

His words feel like a promise of something more and I worry that I'm in too deep to recover if he doesn't catch me when I fall.

CHAPTER 17

Dawson

AFTER A QUICK SHOWER AND ORDERING TAKEOUT FROM a local Thai restaurant, Reese and I are snuggled up on the couch in the living room watching a movie. I can't remember the last time I took a night off—let alone a whole day—but with her, every minute is a precious escape. It's been a while since I've sat down to watch TV, but when Reese found out I haven't seen *Zoolander*, she insisted I watch it. Apparently, my lack of pop culture knowledge was a cry for help requiring an immediate fix.

My back is against the armrest, and Reese is nestled under my arm. Her head rests on my shoulder, legs extended with one knee propped up, and a bowl of popcorn on her lap. I run my fingers gently through her hair, taking in her scent and the rise and fall of her breath.

She plops a piece of popcorn into her mouth and points to the TV, where Derek Zoolander strikes his iconic "Blue Steel" pose.

"This part cracks me up every time I watch it," she says,

erupting into laughter when the camera zooms in on his exaggerated pout. "I forgot how funny this movie is." She giggles harder, clutching her stomach.

God, I'll never get tired of that sound.

I'm completely captivated by her, losing track of the movie as I watch Reese, unguarded and free. Her laugh is contagious, pulling a grin from me as I soak in the sound of her joy.

This place has always been just a house—a stopover between the office and the tattoo shop where I can catch a few hours of sleep and change my clothes. But with Reese here, I can picture it as a home brimming with laughter, love, and warmth.

I shake off the notion as a fleeting fantasy. The idea of someone like me falling in love seems preposterous. I can't even admit that Harrison is my friend, hiding behind our professional dealings because I'm too afraid to trust anyone. That same fear has kept me from committing to a long-term relationship.

Yet, meeting Reese has offered a new perspective, making me wonder if opening up to someone and exploring the possibility of something real wouldn't be so bad.

She has a bright future ahead, and it's hard to believe she'd choose someone like me with a jaded past and who's stuck in his ways. Despite my best efforts to push it aside, an unshakeable thought lingers: I don't think one weekend with her will be enough.

Reese angles her head to study me. "Please tell me you're not bored already," she says with a teasing smile.

I glance between her and the TV screen. "No, I was just thinking about how I want to take you on a trip tomorrow." Now is as good a time as any to break the news to her.

She sets the popcorn bowl on the ground and adjusts her position so we're face-to-face. "We can't leave the city; we have work on Monday."

That's the last thing I want to think about.

"Don't worry. It's just a day trip. We'll be back tomorrow night with plenty of time to prepare for the work week." I hold my breath, my eyes locked on her as she considers my offer.

The silence grows heavier with each passing second, making me second guess my intentions, until her face brightens and she nods in agreement.

"Count me in, but I expect a pumpkin spice latte in the morning. I'll need the extra caffeine for our little adventure, especially if you keep me up late tonight."

I lower my head, pressing a kiss to her lips. "One venti pumpkin spice latte will be waiting for you in the morning... Actually, we'd better make it two because I have big plans for you tonight, Ms. Taylor."

"Looking forward to it, Mr. Tate."

My enthusiasm for tonight pales in comparison to what I have in store for her.

As promised, a pumpkin spice latte was ready for Reese when we boarded the private jet this morning. Though our flight to Aspen Grove was quick, I savored every minute with her curled up beside me.

When we arrive, I exit the plane first, watching as Reese steps off dressed in a gray knit sweater, fitted jeans, and a pair of white sneakers with sunflowers drawn on the sides. She surveys the area, her eyes growing wide with excitement.

The crisp fall air greets us, carrying with it the scent of pine. The trees line the horizon in a patchwork of vibrant orange, red, and yellow, and the ground is dotted with fallen leaves, crunching beneath our feet as we make our way to a black SUV.

"This place is beautiful," she says.

I take her hand as we descend the stairs. "There's nothing like it," I agree.

I've only been to Aspen Grove once for a meeting with Harrison, but it was memorable enough that I knew this was where I wanted to bring Reese.

Harrison steps out of the idling SUV, his sour expression shifting to a pleasant smile when he greets Reese. "Welcome to Aspen Grove," he says, extending his hand. "I'm Harrison, Dawson's friend."

"We're colleagues," I mutter.

"Right, because colleagues go out of their way to do each other favors," he retorts.

"Thank you," Reese chimes in, accepting his handshake. "I was just telling Dawson how beautiful it is here."

"Glad to hear you like it." Harrison grins.

I place my hand on Reese's lower back, shooting Harrison a warning look. His focus on Reese bothers me—she's stunning, but she's with me, and that makes her off-limits.

I open the back door to the SUV and usher Reese inside, sliding in behind her.

"Are you going to tell me what we're doing here?" she questions as she glances out the window.

"It's a surprise, remember?" I take her hand and place it in my lap, intertwining our fingers.

Harrison's parents have a hundred acres of land offering incredible views, and when I asked what we could do, he suggested Reese and I spend the day at their private lake.

We pull away from the airfield, the sound of crunching gravel giving way to the asphalt.

Aspen Grove is a quaint small town, which is evident when we reach Main Street, where residents are strolling past a row of stores like the Bakehouse Bistro, Brew Haven, and Main Street

Market. Each shop is decorated with seasonal pumpkins and cozy autumn displays.

As we pass a park on our left, I spot a woman in floral overalls with blonde hair styled in a halo braid. She's chasing a little girl in red leggings and a pink tutu, her pigtails bouncing as she races after four dogs—one adult and three yappy puppies. The dogs have marbled-pattern coats, long torsos, short legs, and comically large ears, like a cross between an Australian Shepherd and a Corgi.

Harrison pulls off to the side of the road, and rolls down his window. "Marlow, do you need some help?"

The woman glances over, pausing her pursuit to look at Harrison. When she comes closer to the car I notice she has one blue and one green eye.

"Hey, Harrison. I'll get everyone wrangled eventually, but I appreciate the offer."

"Hi, Uncle Harrison." The little girl shouts in our direction, waving with both hands.

"Hey there, ladybug," he answers with a smile. "Having fun?"

She nods vigorously. "Yes! But Waffles, Muffin, Jellybean, and Cheez-It are being bad." She points an accusing finger at the furry culprits, who are now rolling around in a pile of leaves beneath an oak tree.

Harrison chuckles. "At least they're enjoying themselves."

"Yup! Bye, Uncle Harrison," calls the little girl over her shoulder as she joins the dogs in the leaf pile.

"Have fun." He waves to Marlow.

"Thanks. We'll see you at your parents' house for lunch, right?"

"Yeah, Mom would never let me live it down if I didn't stop by before heading back to the city tonight."

"Great, see you there," Marlow says before turning her attention to the little girl.

Harrison glances back at Reese and me as he pulls back onto

the road. "That's Marlow, my soon-to-be sister-in-law, and my niece Lola. They adopted three puppies a few months ago, and it's been quite the adjustment. My brother was already struggling with training one dog, let alone four." He grins. "It's good for him, though. Before Marlow and Waffles came along, he was even grumpier than you, Dawson."

Reese chokes out a laugh, then quickly covers her mouth when she catches me casting Harrison a sharp look.

We all freeze momentarily when his phone's ringtone comes through the car's sound system, the name *Fallon* appearing on the display screen.

He sighs heavily, tapping the end button. "You're testing my patience, Fallon," he grumbles under his breath.

I remember that name. She's the caterer he was looking for the night we were at the club. There's obviously a backstory there, but I decide now isn't the time to press him on it.

We drive the rest of the way in silence, my hand resting on Reese's thigh. I'm looking forward to spending this time with her, free from interruptions and distractions.

"Here we are," Harrison says as he pulls alongside a pristine lake, the surface shimmering under the afternoon sun.

Nestled close to the water's edge is a cozy picnic for two. A blanket is spread out on the grassy shoreline, dotted with plush cushions. Nearby, a wicker basket overflows with fresh fruit, artisanal meats, cheeses, and bread. There's a cooler with chilled sparkling water and a bottle of white sticking out. In the distance, a small boat bobs in the water, completing the serene lakeside escape.

Harrison and his brothers really outdid themselves with the setup.

I climb out of the vehicle and offer my hand to help Reese.

"Have fun, you two," Harrison says from the driver's seat. "I'm going to my parents' house, so just text me when you're ready to head back to the airfield." He gives me a smirk before driving off.

"I can't believe you did all this for me." Reese beams when she gets to the picnic setup.

"Harrison and his family did most of the work," I admit. "I wanted to make sure everything was perfect."

"It is," Reese says. "Thank you, Dawson." She winds her arms around my neck, and I lean down to kiss her.

"I wanted you to have a day where you don't have to do anything but relax, and I figured this was the perfect place to do it."

"You were right."

I lead her to the blanket and once we're seated, I take the paper plates from the basket and serve up a sampling of everything.

"This looks so good," Reese says when I set her plate in front of her.

"Dig in," I encourage.

As we eat, we enjoy the breathtaking view. The midday sun casts a golden light over the tranquil lake. In the reflection off the water's surface you can see the surrounding trees' autumn colors come to life. A gentle breeze sends a few crisp leaves fluttering down to the ground around us. It's a serene setting, one that I'm glad Reese is enjoying.

She's lying on her side, propped up on one elbow—her plate of food on the blanket beside her.

"When are you and Noah planning to take the LSAT?" I'm seated next to her, my back resting against a cushion and my legs stretched out in front of me.

"The second week of January," Reese says with a twinkle in her eye. "Having a block of uninterrupted time to study during the week has been a tremendous help. I can't thank you enough."

I reach over to graze my knuckles across her cheek. "I'll do whatever it takes to help you achieve your dream."

She gives me a grateful smile, popping a piece of cheddar cheese wrapped in prosciutto into her mouth.

"Do you have any law schools in mind you want to apply to?

For the most part, we've avoided talking about the future. No commitments or promises have been made past our time spent together this weekend.

I've deliberately avoided thinking about what would happen if she moved away for law school. It's a real possibility, but that doesn't mean I have to like it. Regardless of how things turn out with Reese, losing her—even if it's down the line—would leave an irreplaceable void.

Reese covers her mouth with her hand while she finishes chewing, then says, "I'd like to stay in New York if possible. It's hard enough only seeing Grams once a week. I don't think either of us could handle living in different states. She might be healthy now, but that could change anytime." She pauses to dab her lips with a napkin. "My grandpa's passing was unexpected and extremely hard on Grams and me."

"What happened?"

She pushes her plate aside and sits up, drawing her legs to her chest. "It was the middle of January. He was in the front yard knocking snow off a tree and had a heart attack. Grams was picking me up from school, and when we got back to the house, an ambulance was leaving with grandpa inside. He died on the way to the hospital." She looks out toward the lake, a flicker of anguish crossing her face. "I miss him so much. Every morning he used to make us breakfast because he said it was the most important meal of the day, and once a week, he brought home flowers for Grams and me to show how much he loved us."

A sharp pain shoots through my chest. "Damn, Reese, I'm sorry you had to go through that." I wrap my arm around her shoulders and press a kiss to her forehead. "He sounds like a wonderful man."

"He was the best," she whispers, leaning against my chest.

I can't begin to grasp the extent of her grief, especially since she was only a teenager when she lost him. One silver lining of being in foster care is that I haven't had to cope with that kind of loss. I never met my biological grandparents or extended family and was therefore spared the pain of losing them. While I haven't experienced this particular brand of suffering, I want to be the person supporting Reese through her worst days.

She lifts her head and smooths out her hair. "Enough about me. What was it like when you first moved in with Martha and Colby?" She stops briefly to study my face. "As long as you're comfortable sharing." she adds cautiously.

I pull my arm away from her shoulders and settle back into my cushion. Reese places her hand on my thigh, patiently waiting for me to speak.

"I was a pain in the ass from the start and refused to come out of my room for the first few weeks. However, Martha was stubborn. She sat outside my closed door for an hour every day and would tell me stories about her childhood, how she met Colby and her love of interior design." I smile fondly at the memory. "I've never told her this, but in those early days, I would sit on the other side of the door and listen while I drew in my sketchbook. Her voice was comforting, and her showing up every day meant more than she'll ever know."

After spending my childhood being passed over for younger kids, it was an adjustment having someone show up for me consistently despite my reluctance.

"I'm lucky Martha and Colby never gave up on me. Everything I've accomplished would never have been possible without them," I say. "They live in Connecticut now, but we talk on the phone at least once a week. In fact, I've told them about you." I add, watching her reaction closely.

"You have?" Reese's voice rises a pitch. "What did you tell them?"

"Oh, just that we made out the night we met, and got a little frisky in my conference room the other day."

"Please tell me you're kidding." She hides her face behind her hands, hoping to mask the color rising in her cheeks.

"Yes, Red, I'm only joking, I promise." My admission gets me a playful swat on the chest, and she narrows her eyes at me with mock irritation.

"What did you really tell them?" she asks.

"I said that you're studying for the LSAT and want to pursue a career in child advocacy. They're not going to let up until they meet you."

"I'd like that." Reese smiles.

Before her, there was never anyone I'd considered introducing to Martha and Colby, but there are a lot of firsts I've found that I'd like to share with her if given the chance.

I wonder what it would be like to have a family with Reese.

The idea comes out of left field, leaving me unsure how to process it. I've never been interested in having a family before. My focus has been on achieving financial success and establishing a reputation as a high-powered attorney. I never wanted to bring a kid into a situation where there was a chance they could experience the same instability I did or be shuffled between two estranged parents.

Now, there's a small part of me that wonders if having a kid with the right person could lead to something positive. I quickly dismiss it, understanding it's something I may want to consider in the future but not right now.

"You're concentrating pretty hard over there," Reese teases, popping a grape into her mouth.

I look over to find her sitting with her legs crossed, watching me intently. She doesn't like staying still for too long; her restless energy and active mind keep her on the move.

I flash her a grin. "I'm just thinking about how this is the best weekend I've had in ages."

She returns my gaze with a content look. "Me too. It's so nice not to worry about having to work at the club or any of my other responsibilities."

I take the chance to broach a topic that I've been waiting to bring up. "I hope you don't mind me asking, but are you planning to keep working at Echo?"

She winces. "Why do you ask?" she questions, nervously tapping her fingers against her thighs.

"You're stretched thin with working at the office and the club, plus studying for the LSAT. I'm worried you're pushing yourself too hard." Her eyes narrow slightly, suggesting she knows I'm holding back. "Honestly, I was hoping the bonus might make you reconsider working at the club." When I notice the unease in her expression I add, "the bonus isn't contingent on you quitting though. "I've seen how important going to law school is for you and want you to have every opportunity to achieve your dream, including making sure you have ample time to study. Martha and Colby were there for me when I was preparing for the LSAT and applying to law schools, and even though you have Noah, I want to be there for you, too."

I open my arm in invitation and without hesitation, Reese snuggles up next to me. She rests her head on my chest and drapes her arm over me.

She glances up at me with a trace of guilt visible in her expression. "I might have already reached out to my supervisor at Echo and told them I'm quitting. He said I'd be missed at the club, but understood. Since the schedule for this upcoming week was still being finalized, he said I could quit effective immediately." She takes a deep breath between continuing. "You were right," she admits as she twirls a piece of hair around her finger. "I've been burning the candle at both ends. My future has to come first, and my best chance of getting into law school is putting my energy into studying and my full-time job. But I'm still having doubts about accepting the bonus. Like I said yesterday, I haven't earned it."

Like hell she hasn't.

"Consider it hazard pay for dealing with my foul moods," I counter. "It's the least I can do for all the late nights you've put in, not to mention the patience you've shown me."

She taps her chin thoughtfully, a playful grin spreading across her face. "When you put it like that, it's hard to argue with your logic," she teases.

"Perfect. I'm glad we've resolved that," I say, making sure there's no space for additional arguments.

The HR team at Thompson & Tate has already been instructed to give a fifteen percent bonus to all support staff as a token of my appreciation for their hard work and dedication to making our firm a continued success. However, I couldn't take a chance that it would be enough to cover all of Reese's expenses.

There was no guarantee she'd agree to quit working at Echo, so I did everything possible to make the choice easier if she declined.

Yesterday, while she was saying goodbye to Georgia after our visit, I waited for her in the reception area of Oak Ridge. I asked the person working at the front desk for the administrator's contact information. They were reluctant at first but relented when I told them I wanted to make a significant donation to the facility.

Within ten minutes, I had spoken to the administrator, and had my financial advisor wire ten million dollars to cover the expenses of all residents at the facility for the next year. Plus, I gave him specific instructions to order enough cashmere blankets for two to be delivered to each resident at the facility. The idea of Georgia getting cold at night is unacceptable.

If Reese finds out it was me, she'll have a hard time staying upset with me since I did something that benefits all the residents, not just her grandmother.

Replacing her furnace while we were gone would have been easy, but then she might have wanted to go back home tonight. I'm hoping I can persuade her to stay with me for one more night, though if I have it my way, it'll be for much longer.

Reese's body relaxes against mine as she looks up at the sky. "This place is so beautiful. Thanks for bringing me here, Dawson," she says with a smile.

"Anything for you," I vow.

She might think they're empty words, but I'm serious. There's nothing I wouldn't do to make her smile like that again.

"It's too bad we have to go back to reality tomorrow." She sighs, her tone despondent.

What if we don't have to? At least not entirely.

An idea begins to form as I consider the best way to implement it.

It's become clear that one weekend with her isn't enough, and I'm determined to find a way to make her mine for the long haul.

CHAPTER 18

Reese

I WAKE UP TO THE SUN STREAMING THROUGH THE WINDOW. I'm draped across Dawson's chest with my head nestled in the crook of his shoulder, leg hitched over his thigh, and his arm wrapped securely around my waist. When we returned from Aspen Grove last night, we came back to his place.

This past weekend was like something out of a fairytale… if the storybook hero was a grumpy lawyer covered in tattoos with a heart of gold.

Aspen Grove was stunning, and I enjoyed meeting Harrison. He and Dawson seem to be cut from the same cloth: rough around the edges but fiercely loyal to the people they care about. Dawson is reluctant to admit it, but their loyalty to each other runs deeper than business associates, and I'm glad he has a friend like Harrison in his corner.

I shift slightly, tilting my head to gaze at Dawson. His eyes remain shut, and his features appear more relaxed than usual. The creases around his eyes are gone, and he looks like the weight of the world has been lifted.

He cracks one eye open, a lazy smile forming. "Like what you see, Red?"

"Hmm, I've seen better."

"Is that so?" He cups the back of my neck, tugging me closer as he plunges his tongue past my lips. I'm breathless when he pulls away with a smirk on his face. "Last night you seemed to rather enjoy yourself, considering you were screaming my name while my cock was buried inside your pussy."

I playfully push him away. "That mouth is going to get you in trouble one of these days."

"It served me well last night," he says quietly, and my cheeks flush red.

When I glance over at the clock on the nightstand I panic when I see that it's already 6:15.

"Oh, shoot. I have to get going." I scramble to get out of bed, but Dawson doesn't let me get very far—pulling me back into his arms and showering my shoulder with kisses.

"What are you doing?" I question, flustered. "It'll take me at least an hour to get to my place and another forty-five minutes to get to the office. If I don't leave now, I'll be late."

"Good thing you're sleeping with the boss," he quips.

I poke him in the rib, giving him a mock scowl. "That's not funny, *Mr. Tate.*"

He conceals a smirk, pressing a kiss to my lip in apology. "You can go straight to the office from here. Don't worry, we'll leave at different times if you're worried about someone seeing us together."

"As much as I'd like that, I didn't bring any office-appropriate clothes with me." I motion to my backpack in the corner, where yesterday's outfit is tossed on top.

He gives me a smug grin. "Why don't you check the closet?"

My eyes narrow. "Dawson, what did you do?"

He settles back on his pillow, his hands propped up behind his head. "You'll have to see for yourself."

I release a frustrated sigh. He's been around me enough to know that patience isn't one of my strong suits. Dawson lets me climb out of bed this time, and I grab his white dress shirt hanging from the armchair on my way to the closet.

"You look good in my clothes," he growls, a possessive glint in his eye.

"I'm glad we agree—this shirt looks way better on me, doesn't it." I toss him a wink.

With his attention fixed on me, I cross the room, swaying my hips with every step knowing that he's enjoying the show.

When I enter the massive walk-in closet, I find one side is meticulously organized with a large selection of tailored suits, crisp dress shirts, and pressed pants. There's even a full panel of shelves filled to the brim with polished shoes arranged by color and style.

My gaze is drawn to the opposite side of the closet. It's empty except for a single outfit on gold hangers: a cream-colored cashmere sweater with a fitted silhouette, a burgundy pencil skirt, and a pair of nude heels on the ground below.

As I'm running my hand down the luxurious fabric of the sweater, I sense Dawson's presence behind me. He circles his arms around my waist and presses a kiss to my head.

"I take it you like your outfit?"

"It's lovely. When did you have it delivered?"

"Yesterday, while we were in Aspen Grove," he explains. "And before you thank me, I should tell you, it was all for my benefit."

I angle my head to look up at him with a bemused smile. "Is that so?"

"Absolutely," he states proudly. "I wanted more time with you this morning and I figured this was the best way to make it happen."

When I spin around to face him, Dawson is standing in his

boxers, his blue eyes glued to me. The bold lines of his tattoos only add to his sex appeal, and it's almost sinful how attractive he is after rolling out of bed.

"Is that the only reason?"

He winds his hand around my lower back to draw me closer. "I was hoping to convince you to stay with me again tonight..." He pauses, waiting until I look up at him to continue. "I don't want things to go back to the way they were, Red."

Neither do I.

But it's not that simple.

"Dawson, this past weekend with you has been great... incredible, actually."

One of the most unforgettable experiences I've ever had.

"But you're still my boss." I frown, slumping my shoulders in resignation. "We've obliterated every professional boundary there is, and I'm not sure what comes next."

Dawson runs his hands along my arms in soothing strokes. "I have one question for you. Do you want me? Because if the answer is yes, I'll find a way around the non-fraternization policy. Being the boss wouldn't be worth shit if I didn't have the power to bend the rules now, would it?"

I scrunch my nose, unsure of how feasible his plan is. If it were that easy to change the policies, something tells me he would have done it already.

"We're in over our heads." I sigh, scrubbing my hand across my face.

"You didn't answer the question. Do. You. Want. Me?" he asks again, deliberately enunciating every word.

Do I want him?

The question lingers in my mind as I contemplate our situation. Dawson has embedded himself into my life and my heart, and it feels like there's no hope of unraveling the complex web of emotions we've spun. We've bound by forces we can't control and I want to hold on to this feeling and never let it go.

"I want you, Dawson…"

More than anything.

"But I'm barely making ends meet, and with law school in my future, my life is only going to get more complicated." I wring my hands together. "You're a successful lawyer with a prestigious practice—why would you settle for someone with an uncertain future?"

Dawson scoffs like he's offended by my comment. "I hate to break it to you, angel, but you're wrong. I'd be damn lucky to call you mine." He lifts my chin, and the fire in his eyes steals my breath. "You have a kind heart, and a gift for making everyone around you feel special. I might not deserve you, but that won't stop me from showing why we belong together."

His resolve makes my pulse race, and he makes me feel more alive and cherished than I thought possible. Every moment spent with him is better than the last. It's the lingering doubt that causes me to hesitate, knowing that once we commit there's no going back.

"What if things between us don't work out?" I whisper.

The unspoken questions hover in the space between us. *What happens to my job if someone finds out? What if you decide that you don't want me anymore? What if this was all for nothing?*

"All I'm asking is for you to give us a chance because I'm not ready for this to end." He clasps my hands in his and rests his forehead against mine. "I can't predict the future, but I promise that whatever comes, we'll do it together."

I'm overcome by a soothing sense of calm as warmth spreads through my chest. Not only do I believe him, but I'm reassured that this thing between us means more to him than a weekend fling or a casual encounter with someone from the office.

"Okay," I agree.

"You mean it?" Dawson asks.

He breathes a sigh of relief as I nod and bends down to kiss me.

Now that I've had a glimpse of what it's like to be totally and completely his, I can't imagine settling for anything less. Dawson has shattered my previous notions of what a relationship could be like, leaving me yearning for the affection only he can provide. It feels like I'm on a roller coaster without brakes—terrifying and thrilling.

The last few days since our return from our trip to Aspen Grove have been surreal. It feels like I'm walking on a cloud, lost in a state of contentment. I haven't been back to my place yet, and for a little while longer, I'd like to live in the fantasy that Dawson and I have all the time in the world.

I'm studying in Dawson's conference room when my laptop pings with a message.

> **Grace:** I had so much fun at lunch yesterday! It was nice to get out of the office for a change.
>
> **Reese:** Thanks for inviting me!

Now that I'm no longer working at Echo, I have more free time to study at night and on the weekends, which means I can afford to take an actual lunch break every now and then. Grace and I went to a pizza place down the street yesterday. It was nice to take a break from the office and catch up in person since most of our interactions have been through the team chat system.

> **Grace:** Took your advice and tried a pumpkin latte this morning.

Reese: What did you think?

Grace: So good!

Reese: I know right! They're my favorite.

Grace: I'm totally hooked.

Grace: Heads up. I saw Rob earlier and he's in one of his moods.

Reese: Thanks for letting me know.

Grace: Running late for a meeting. Talk soon.

Reese: Have a great rest of your day!

Grace: You too!

I only have thirty minutes before I have to go back to my desk, so I shut my laptop and return to studying.

Soon after, I hear the door open and glance up from my LSAT book. "I thought you had a lunch meeting with—" I stop speaking when I see Rob standing in the doorway, his expression as cold as ice.

"Rob?" His name comes out as a question. "What are you doing?"

Dawson's conference room is off-limits to the rest of the staff and only available if he schedules a meeting with them.

"A better question is, what are *you* doing here?" Rob snaps. "It's past one o'clock and you're supposed to be filing paperwork for the Nelson project." His booming voice fills the room, causing me to tremble. "What the hell is all this anyway?" He storms toward me, yanking my book out of my hand. "You're studying on company time? Give me one good reason I shouldn't fire you and have security see you out."

I stand up to face him, and raise my chin defiantly, my eyes shining with determination. "Dawson gave me permission to study in here. If you have concerns you can take it up with him."

"*Dawson*, is it?" He scoffs. "Getting a little cozy with the boss, aren't we?" He lowers his voice. "I'm sure you're aware of our non-fraternization policy. I'd hate to think what might happen if HR got wind of a rumor that you two are an item."

I maintain a neutral expression, not giving him any leverage. "Rob, you need to go." I point to the hallway. "I'll let you know when I've finished filing the paperwork."

As I reach for my things, I'm startled when Rob steps in front of me, placing himself between me and the table.

He shoves a pudgy finger in my face. "I'm sick and tired of you thinking you can do whatever you want. You're just a paralegal and it's your job to assist *me*."

I ball my hands into fists, refusing to back down. One thing I've learned over the past couple of months is how to be bolder, and to stand my ground when my boundaries are tested. I'm done letting Rob treat me with disrespect, and refuse to cower to his intimidation tactics any longer.

"I'm not *just* a paralegal; I'm a professional. Maybe if you treated me with respect, I'd be more inclined to prioritize your projects."

His jaw visibly tightens. "Why you little—"

"Rob, what the hell are you doing here?" Dawson's voice startles me, and I glance over to where he's standing in the doorway, his gaze narrowing in on Rob. "Step back," he growls. "You've crossed a line."

If we weren't in the office with people milling around in the hallway, I doubt Dawson would be this calm.

"I was reminding Reese of her place," Rob sneers. "She seems to have forgotten that she doesn't get special privileges, like an extended lunch break."

Dawson strides toward Rob, who shrinks back until he hits

the wall with nowhere else to go. He gulps loudly as Dawson crowds his space. "Let's get something straight. I've had enough of your antics." Dawson's voice is low and menacing. "The only reason you're working here is because of your uncle. Your track record as a lawyer is unimpressive and I've had enough," he states curtly. "You've lost the privilege of having a paralegal report directly to you."

"What? You can't do that." Rob sputters. "I'm entitled to my own team."

My gaze darts between them. Dawson's fists are clenched at his sides, his posture rigid, and the vein in his neck pulses. Rob tries to mask his unease, but the sweat on his brow is a clear giveaway that he's scared shitless.

Dawson raises a brow. "Wrong, Rob. You *earn* that privilege and you haven't proven yourself capable of managing anyone."

I put my hand over my mouth, stifling the surprising urge to laugh. It's poetic justice to see him getting a taste of his own medicine.

Rob shoves past Dawson, throwing my textbook on the table. "You won't get away with this," he shouts at Dawson. "You only got where you are through manipulation and exploiting others. You're going to pay for what you did to my uncle."

Dawson folds his arms across his chest, his gaze cold. "I'd think very carefully about your next words, Rob. I'm not someone who takes a threat lightly." He projects dominance, and it's such a turn-on to watch him in action.

Rob scoffs, though I don't miss his hands trembling. "You think you're invincible, but you're not. You'll see." He doesn't wait around before bolting from the room.

A group of employees has gathered to see what's going on, but as soon as Dawson scowls at them they disperse, returning to their desks.

I throw away the container from my lunch and collect my textbook.

Dawson positions himself between me and the door, blocking me from view. His concern is evident. There's no doubt he'd go to any length to keep me safe.

He watches me closely as he adjusts his cufflinks. "Are you okay?"

"I'm fine," I say, running my finger along the crease in his brow. "Rob's nothing more than a loudmouth bully who's all talk and no action."

Dawson pushes a piece of hair from my face. "Mark my words that asshole will pay for how he's treated you. I'll make sure he doesn't bother you again."

I run my hand along his arm, making sure it's out of sight from the hallway. "Thank you," I murmur.

"Are you staying at my place tonight?" He keeps his voice low.

"Dawson, you can't talk like that at the office." My voice comes out breathless.

He grazes my collarbone with a slow, deliberate touch, his finger trailing to my lips as he studies my mouth. His back faces the door and if anyone was still lingering in the hall all they'd see is Dawson towering over me. "You better get back to work, Ms. Taylor. We wouldn't want to fuel any rumors now would we?" He smirks before pulling away.

I nod, and he squeezes my hand gently before striding out of the conference room.

I'm overcome with a sense of peace. Ever since my grandpa passed, the weight of my responsibilities has only grown heavier, making it feel impossible to manage on my own. But now with Dawson in my life, I'm learning to accept that I don't have to do it all alone. He's shown me that there's strength in vulnerability and letting someone support me, and help me through both the good and bad.

Before I leave the conference room, I check my phone, smiling when I see a message from Noah.

Noah: Want to go to brunch on Saturday before we study?

Noah: It'll be my treat.

Reese: Sounds great. I've missed you.

I'm looking forward to seeing him so we can catch up. We constantly text and talk on the phone, but haven't seen each other in person since Dawson showed up at the club. I've avoided bringing it up because it's a conversation I'd prefer to have face-to-face.

Noah: I've missed you too babe.

Noah: I'll meet you there at 11.

Reese: Can't wait.

He's going to want an update on Dawson and me, especially since I quit at the club without an explanation. Honestly, I'm not sure how to explain it. Dawson and I haven't defined whatever this thing is between us or talked about our next steps.

What I do know is that I don't want it to end.

When I enter The Sunny Egg, a breakfast café in Midtown, I'm greeted with the aroma of freshly ground coffee beans and toasted pastries. They host a weekend brunch, so the place is packed.

I spot Noah waving at me from a booth in the back corner. I'm looking forward to catching up, not so much to the interrogation I suspect he has planned. How do I explain that I spent a weekend at my boss's place, and every night since?

During this past work week Dawson and I went back to his

place after we finished at the office. Most nights we don't get there until late, but we still curl up on the couch with a bowl of popcorn while we watch a movie. He hasn't seen many, so I've introduced him to a few classics in a variety of genres including *How to Lose a Guy in Ten Days, The Avengers, and The Hangover.*

Those peaceful moments with him, when it's just the two of us at his place, make me see that I'm more at risk of falling in love with him than ever before.

The logical side of my brain recognizes that there's much more at stake than the mutual attraction between two people. My job is on the line, and there's no guarantee of a happy ending. Yet, my heart isn't interested in being rational—it only wants Dawson, no matter the cost.

"Look who finally showed up," Noah says, giving me a teasing smirk as I approach our table.

"I'm only five minutes late," I say, leaning across the table to hug him.

"Yes, but you're usually ten minutes early." He quirks a smug brow. "You look stunning in that dress," He gestures to my outfit, effectively changing the subject. "Is it new?"

I narrow my eyes at him. He knows full well that my wardrobe consists of six dresses and three skirts I've had on rotation since my freshman year of college.

Since we returned from Aspen Grove, Dawson has arranged for a high-end dress or outfit in my size and preferred style to be delivered every morning. He must have guessed I'd decline a shopping spree or an entirely new wardrobe, but I haven't been able to bring myself to reject his thoughtful gifts, especially not this stunning dress.

It has a flattering A-line cut with buttons running down the front, and I paired it with sneakers that I doodled pink and navy-blue flowers on.

Noah drums his fingers against the table as he watches me. "What's going on, Reese? What aren't you telling me?"

"I'm not answering any questions until I've had my coffee," I complain, noticing two cups on his side of the table.

While I try to limit my caffeine intake, I'm not fully functional until I've had caffeine. Unfortunately, this morning I didn't have time to get a cup before I rushed out the door.

"Here you go." Noah grins, sliding one of the cups toward me. "It's a pumpkin spice latte, just the way you like it. I also ordered you avocado toast with a side of eggs and fruit."

"You're relentless," I say, lifting the warm cup and savoring my first sip. "But just because you're bribing me with my favorite brunch doesn't mean I'll tell you anything."

"I'll take my chances. I'm willing to offer an information exchange, and something tells me you'll want to hear what I have to share."

I shoot him a sidelong glance as I take another sip. Noah leans back in his seat, a knowing smirk on his lips. It's only a matter of time before I give in—he's well aware of my impatience, and I'm already on the edge of my seat, itching to find out what he has to share.

Before I can reply, a server brings over our food.

"Here you are." I practically salivate when she places my plate in front of me.

"Thanks. This looks amazing," Noah tells her.

"My pleasure," she says before hurrying off.

When Noah reaches for his fork, I lean forward to grab his wrist. "There will be plenty of time to eat later. What did you want to tell me?"

He chuckles as he sets his fork down. "I knew you wouldn't be able to hold out."

"Yeah, yeah." I wave him off. "Spill the beans."

"The night Mr. Tall, Dark, and Handsome showed up at the

club and you were both off doing who knows what, David showed up," Noah says. "Turns out the bar was running low on tequila, so he dropped off a crateful."

My eyes widen. "Oh my god. Noah, why didn't you say anything before?"

David is the general manager at the club and usually works the dayshift. I can't believe Dawson and I were in that man's office doing unspeakable things. There's no question he would have fired me if he'd walked in on us. And Dawson would have made matters worse by trying to defend me.

Not that it matters since I'm no longer working there. The HR department at Thomspon & Tate sent an email to all its paralegals this past week about the substantial bonus we'd be receiving. It's far more than I expected and while it still feels like charity, it makes me feel better that we'll all benefit from Dawson's generosity.

"Don't worry, babe. The second David started for his office, I intercepted him," Noah assures me.

"What did you do?" I ask.

He shrugs. "Asked him out."

I pause mid-sip, my coffee cup hovering in the air. "You what? In case you forgot, he's your boss." Technically, our interactions with him are limited to receiving our schedule via text or email, but still.

Noah raises an eyebrow with a playful grin. "You're one to talk. There isn't a non-fraternization policy at the club, so I figured why not." He shrugs. "The worst thing he could have said was no." He flashes a grin over his cup. "Apparently, he's been into me for a while now but wasn't sure if you and I were dating so he never made a move."

"Sorry I inadvertently cock-blocked you," I tease.

"Don't worry about it," he says as he tosses a blueberry into his mouth. "Now are you going to tell me what's going on with you and Dawson? That man clearly has it bad for you. I've never seen someone so territorial over a woman before."

My cheeks grow hot under his scrutiny. "He surprised me with a trip to Aspen Grove."

"Are you serious? I've heard that place is gorgeous."

"It really is," I agree.

I take a bite of the eggs, savoring the butter flavor melting on my tongue. When I glance up Noah is staring at me.

"You can't tell me you went out of town with the guy and then leave me hanging. Why aren't you driving off into the sunset?"

I playfully toss my napkin at him. "You watch too many Hallmark movies. In case you've forgotten, Dawson is my boss, which complicates things since we *do* have a non-fraternization policy. Not to mention he's twelve years older than me. I'm finding it hard to believe he'd want to tie himself to someone whose financials are a mess." I sigh and push my fruit around on my plate. "Seriously, Noah, I'm looking at three years of law school and am still planning on choosing the career path that pays far less than what I'd make at a corporate firm."

"It's convenient that the man is a billionaire then, isn't it." He smirks. "I'm sure he'll be happy to take care of you."

I burst out laughing. "It's probably not true."

"I'm serious. Rumor is he took a gamble on some high-risk stocks that paid off, and combined with his firm's success, he's sitting on a goldmine." Noah lets out a low whistle.

My laughter fades, giving away to a furrowed brow when I recall the articles I found online when I was looking up Dawson online that suggested otherwise. I figured Dawson was rich since he's the managing partner of a prominent law firm, but I didn't think he was *that* rich. Not that the money is important to me regardless.

I remember a conversation where he mentioned Harrison

being a billionaire and emphasized the importance of not judging a book by its cover. Could he have been referring to himself?

In reality, he's the most generous person I know. He only does pro bono work at Steel & Ink, makes sure his employees are well taken care of, looks out for Christian and his mom, and is constantly looking for ways to make my life easier.

Noah reaches out to place his hand over mine, pulling my focus back to him. "Sometimes the best things in life aren't planned, and the greatest risk is not daring to take a chance. If you're not willing to take a leap of faith you'll never know what you could be missing out on."

"Since when did you become a philosopher?" I tease.

"I'm feeling rather inspired today," he says with a twinkle in his eye.

As we go back to eating our breakfast, I think about what he said. Falling for Dawson wasn't part of the plan, and until he came along, I had sworn off men. But now it occurs to me that by embracing the unexpected, I've found someone who makes me feel at home again.

CHAPTER 19

Dawson

THE PAST WEEK WITH REESE HAS BEEN AMAZING. EVERY morning, I wake up with her in my arms and I watch her eyes light up when she checks the closet to find what new outfit I've had delivered. Nothing brings me more satisfaction than seeing her smile, and it makes me want to find a new way to make sure it never fades.

It's been a long day at the office and I'm counting down the hours until Reese and I can go home.

Our home.

We haven't talked about her staying long-term, but I love the idea of making it permanent.

Before I start reviewing the contract waiting for me on my desk, I take out my phone and shoot Harrison a text. When I asked for his help in setting up a date with Reese in Aspen Grove, I hadn't expected him to go all out. Guess when you ask the Staffords for a favor, they take it seriously.

Dawson: Thanks again for your help. Reese loved visiting Aspen Grove.

Harrison: No problem. That's what friends are for.

I'm about to remind him that I only asked because he owed me a favor and that we're not friends, but I hesitate. Would it really be so bad to have another person willing to help me out in a bind, no questions asked? Even without the favor, I get the feeling Harrison would have helped—albeit reluctantly.

Dawson: You ever going to tell me what happened with Fallon at the club?

Harrison: I have to go. I'm heading into a board meeting.

Dawson: I'll take that as a no.

I doubt his night ended like it did for Reese and me. Fallon was giving him an earful, not letting him get a word in edgewise. Harrison never did explain what happened between them in the first place, but from what I saw it seems like there was a lot left unresolved.

As I'm putting my phone away, Maxwell Thompson, the founding partner of Thomson & Tate, and Rob's uncle, bursts into my office. He's the last person I expected to see today.

After he nearly brought the company to its knees a few years ago, I prohibited him from coming into the office. All our communications are strictly via email and occasionally over the phone. Technically he's still a partner and has a say in the day-to-day operations, but he's not permitted to go near the finances, or handle client communications.

When I discovered he'd been embezzling funds, my initial instinct was to expose him, but I knew the fallout for the firm would be irreversible. And he refused to give up his part in the company.

I turn away from my computer and rest my hands on my desk. "Maxwell, what are you doing here?"

"Demanding your resignation," he snarls.

I let out a humorless laugh. "Is that so?"

"Damn right it is. You practically ripped my company out from under my feet. Did you really think I would just let it go?" He slams his fist on my desk. "I've been biding my time until I could strike back and take my rightful place at the helm, with Rob as a managing partner."

I let out a dry laugh. "Rob can't even manage his own work-load, let alone run a firm. Not to mention his treatment of his co-workers is an HR disaster waiting to happen." I sit up straight in my chair. "You better have some damning evidence against me if you're planning to oust me."

"Oh, I do." He slams a dossier on the desk.

I eye the folder suspiciously. It was only a matter of time before he tried pulling a stunt like this. He probably figured that if he waited long enough, I'd become complacent and let my guard down.

He was wrong.

Maxwell grits his teeth when I don't move to inspect the folder. The sweat on his brow betrays his rising unease that his plan isn't having the impact he expected. After several seconds of staring me down he finally caves, opening the file himself and shoving a picture toward me. It's a street view of Steel & Ink. I'm standing out front talking to Mickey. It's summertime, and my sleeves are rolled up, revealing my tattoos.

"You've been having me followed." I state. For at least a year, based on when this was taken." I motion to the photo.

"Are you forgetting I'm the one who taught you the impor-tance of gathering intel?"

I shake my head, keeping my hands clasped. "No, but I hope that's not all you've got. You're a bigger fool than I realized if you think threatening me over a few tattoos is going to get me to quit."

"I figured you might say that." A sadistic smile crosses his

lips as he sinks into the chair across from mine. He flips to another picture in the folder and taps it for emphasis. "What about
fraternizing with your paralegal? Your much *younger* paralegal?
Is that enough incentive for you?"

Son of a bitch.

A low growl escapes my lips. The photo is of me and Reese
holding hands, and she's lifting on her toes to kiss me. It was
taken the day we went to visit Georgia, right after we left Oak
Ridge.

"This is rather damning, wouldn't you say?" Maxwell
taunts, his expression full of satisfaction. "If word gets out that
you're fucking your paralegal, you'll both be finished," he warns,
his tone threatening.

I stay still, my eyes narrowing on him. "What is it you want
Max?"

"Like I said, for you to resign immediately." He sounds
pleased with himself.

"You do remember the firm was hemorrhaging money
when you hired me, right? Who's to say that won't happen again
when I'm gone? Our highest profitable clients are ones *I've*
brought in and they are loyal to me."

When Maxwell brought me on as a first-year attorney, the
firm was in a dire state. Their history of unresolved client dis-
putes and frequent litigation losses was well-known. Despite
having offers from other respectable firms, I was drawn to the
challenge, and saw an opportunity to make myself indispens-
able if I could help turn their reputation around.

It soon became evident that information was the key to
gaining power and winning cases. With nothing to lose, and a
faulty moral compass, I leveraged that to set myself up for success. Within a record five years, I made partner.

When I uncovered Maxwell's corrupt business dealings, I
demanded that most of the senior partners be fired and replaced

with attorneys who were willing to work to make Thompson & Tate a reputable firm. Now, I have a decision to make—prepare for a complicated legal battle to maintain all the progress I've made or take a risk and venture out on my own.

I open the bottom drawer of my desk and pull out a dossier of my own. It's the ace card I've been holding on to, waiting for the right opportunity to play it.

"You're not the only one who's done his research." I slide the documents toward Maxwell. "You've been busy. Tell me, Max, does your family know you've been gambling with their inheritance or that you sold the beach house in the Hamptons? Something tells me they wouldn't be happy if they found out." I pull out another folder and place it on top of the other.

"What is that?" he demands.

A smirk crosses my lips knowing that I've got him right where I want him. "This little old thing?" I hold up the two-inch-thick binder. "It's a collection of all your misdeeds, and your nephew's too. It turns out Rob is like you in more ways than one." I flip open the folder and push it toward Maxwell.

After my confrontation with Rob last week, I had my team start digging into his background. I should have done it sooner. I've wanted him out for a while now, but his treatment of Reese was the last nail in his coffin, and he's lucky I didn't leave him with a broken nose to match his reputation. No one messes with my woman and gets away with it. Especially not a privileged trust fund brat who's never earned anything in his life.

Whether she admits it or not, Reese Taylor is mine, and I'll go to any lengths to keep her safe. She deserves nothing less.

Maxwell hesitantly riffles through the dossier, his eyes growing round with shock as he scans each page. When he's finished, he rips a handful of the documents from the binder and tosses them to the floor. "How dare you," he shouts. "I should never have let a lowlife posing as a lawyer into my firm."

"But you did," I remind him, my lips curving into a sickly sweet smile. "And now it's time to finally pay the consequences." I slide another stack of documents toward Maxwell. "I'm leaving the company, but this is the list of clients that are coming with me." I nod toward the top page.

His eyes widen as he scans the long list. "This is almost every high-profile client we have." When he gets to the second page, his jaw drops. "You expect me to waive our employees' non-disclosure agreements so they can join your new firm? You can't be serious."

I lean back in my chair with my hands behind my head, soaking in the satisfaction of having the upper hand. "Try to stop me, and I'll leak all the evidence that I've been collecting. I'm sure your family, friends, and colleagues would be interested to hear what kind of lowlife *you* are. Your weaselly nephew too." He glares at me when I place a pen in front of him.

"This is your last chance. If you don't approve my buyout agreement, client transfers, and waive the non-disclosures for our employee, every major news outlet in the city will have the dossier I put together before you've left the building."

Maxwell hesitates, realizing that there's no getting out of this unscathed. He finally bends forward as he reads through and signs each document. With every passing second, his face flushes crimson, betraying his growing agitation. When he finishes signing the last page, he throws the pen down in fury.

"I hope you're happy about single-handedly dismantling this firm," He spits out.

"I've never felt better," I respond, grinning devilishly. "Don't forget, Maxwell, you're the one who said you wanted me to resign."

"Dawson, I have the contract you—" Reese stops short in the doorway when she spots Maxwell. "I'm sorry, sir, I can come back later." She throws me a sideways glance.

I shake my head. "Stay. Mr. Thompson was just leaving."

Maxwell glares at Reese before storming out and slamming my office door behind him.

"What's going on?" she asks. "I heard raised voices and saw that you didn't have any meetings scheduled. I wanted to make sure everything was okay."

I get up from my chair, meeting her halfway across the room.

"Were you worried about me, Ms. Taylor?" I ask, my tone teasing.

I wind my arm around her waist, kissing her deeply, groaning with satisfaction when she slips her tongue inside my mouth.

Every kiss we've shared has led to this one—all-consuming, ravenous, passionate. Nothing feels better than having her secured in my arms. There's no chance I'm letting her go and I want everyone to know that Reese Taylor belongs to me.

She breaks our connection, breathless, and places her hand on my chest. "Dawson, we have to stop. We're at work" she reminds me. "Who just stormed out of your office?"

"That was Maxwell Thompson, the firm's founding partner." She's seen his name on paperwork, but has never met him in person. "He hired a PI to follow me and tried blackmailing me with photos of us outside of Oak Ridge, Georgia's assisted living facility."

Reese's face goes pale, her hand flying to her mouth. "Oh my god, this can't be happening. We shouldn't have been so reckless; this could ruin everything." Her eyes are glassy and unfocused as her gaze darts between me and the door.

I place my hand on her shoulder to reassure her, turning her to look at me. "Reese, everything is going to be okay, I promise." I cup her cheek, waiting until her focus is on me. "Maxwell underestimated me. Both he and Rob have been doing things they shouldn't, and I've been collecting evidence to use when the opportunity presented itself."

Reese tugs her bottom lip between her teeth, processing the news. "What if one of them reports us to HR and they fire me? My chances of going to law school will be ruined, and I won't have enough money to pay for Grams's care. I can't believe I've been so stupid." A tear forms and slides down her cheek, and my chest tightens at the sight.

"Red, I'd never allow that to happen." I wipe away the tear and kiss her forehead. "I'd walk out before I let our relationship tarnish your reputation." I suppress the amused smile that tugs at the corner of my mouth. "In fact, that's exactly what I did."

Reese snaps her gaze to meet mine, her mouth slightly parted "What do you mean?"

I shrug. "I quit, and I'm taking my clients with me." I motion to the list on the desk. "At the new firm, we'll adopt a more lenient policy on relationships in the workplace. We'll have to sign a consensual relationship agreement, and you'll have a different boss, but it's a small price to pay to balance our personal and professional lives."

Reese's expression is unreadable as she processes the news. "How long have you been planning this?"

"I initially intended to have Maxwell removed from the company when the chance presented itself.; however, over the past few weeks, I realized that a clean slate would be a better solution. Starting a new firm would give me more control over policies and how things are run."

"Why wouldn't you tell me about it?"

"You've been dealing with a lot, and I wanted to finalize things before I asked you to move in with me."

Her eyes widen and she takes a step back. "Hold on. Dawson, we've just started seeing each other. I'm not moving in with you."

"Why not?" I ask, making an effort to maintain a calm demeanor. "You've stayed at my place every night since we got back from Aspen Grove. What's the difference?"

Despite her initial protest, I've come up with every excuse to keep her from spending the night at her place, and it's worked so far. I refuse to let her live in a freezing cold house that's crumbling around her when she can stay with me at my place with heated floors and reliable hot water. Having her stay with me means she's safe, comfortable, and right where she belongs—in my arms.

Reese sighs, rubbing her temples. "Since the day I started working at Thompson & Tate, you've called the shots. First you reassigned me to work with you, encouraged me to quit working at Echo, and now I find out you've quit the firm and decided that I'm coming with you. You should have talked to me about it first." She folds her arms across her chest, locking eyes with me. "I'm grateful for everything you've done, but I can't be in a relationship where all the decisions are made for me. I need someone who will consult with me and ask for my input before making major choices that impact me. Otherwise, we're setting ourselves up for failure."

My initial confidence gives way to guilt as I come to understand that my well-meaning actions may have caused Reese more harm than good.

For so long, I've faced challenges head on making choices based on my own judgment. But I failed to adapt and include Reese in choices that affect us both.

I swallow hard. "Damn, you're right. I've been so focused on what I thought was best that I inadvertently kept you out of the decision-making process. There's no excuse for that and I'm so sorry, Reese." My voice is low, weighed down by guilt. "You mean everything to me, and there's nothing more I want than for us to be together. I love waking up next to you every morning, and falling asleep with you in my arms. So much that I wanted to do whatever it took to make sure a future together was possible without disrupting your plans to go to law school."

"I'm enjoying our time together too, Dawson, I'm just not sure if moving in together right now is—" A knock on the door interrupts her mid-sentence.

"I'll get rid of whoever it is," I say, but before I can move Reese is already halfway to the door. "Where are you going?"

"I'm assuming Maxwell wants us out of the building by the end of the day so I better go pack my desk," she says with a tentative smile.

As much as I'd like to drop everything and finish our conversation, she's right. I might have gotten my way, but that won't stop Maxwell from sending security if I'm not out of here by tonight.

"Why don't you take the rest of the day off?" I suggest. "And we can talk more later tonight?"

"Don't you need help here?" Reese asks.

I shake my head. "I've got it covered," I assure her.

As much as I want her here with me, she deserves the chance to process everything. Asking her to move in felt right in the moment, but I didn't consider how overwhelming it might be for her. All I can hope is that once we talk things through, she can forgive me for my shortcomings because nothing else matters if I lose her in the end.

"Okay," Reese says hesitantly. "Only if you're sure."

"Positive."

I give her hand a squeeze on her way out, and it takes every ounce of willpower to stand by when she opens the door to reveal Jeremey standing on the other side with his hand raised, ready to knock again.

Reese slips past him into the hallway, disappearing from view.

"What is it?" I snap.

His face visibly pales as he hands over a report for the Irving project. "You asked me to bring this to you as soon as possible, sir."

"Thanks," I say, taking the report from his hand. "Why don't you step into my office. There's something I want to talk to you about."

There's nothing I'd like to do more than finish my conversation with Reese. But for now, I've got a long list of employees and clients I need to speak with, and an office to pack before Maxwell tries to have security kick me out.

I glance at my watch, noting that I only have a few hours until I'm supposed to be at the tattoo shop. With everything going on, I should cancel my appointments, but I could use the distraction, especially if I don't hear back from Reese by then.

CHAPTER 20

Reese

AFTER MY CONVERSATION WITH DAWSON WAS CUT SHORT, I packed up my things. Luckily, it was during lunchtime so no one was around to ask questions. He mentioned he was bringing some of the staff with him to his new firm, but I assume he has to get an office set up first.

My mind is spinning, trying to make sense of the sudden changes in my life—I'm no longer employed at Thompson & Tate, and Dawson just asked me to move in with him. It's a lot to process.

I appreciate his suggestion to take the rest of the day off. He could sense that I was overwhelmed and needed time to sort through it all.

The only problem? I realized as I gathered up all my personal items, I wasn't sure where to go. I haven't agreed to move in with Dawson, but also wasn't ready to go back to my place just yet.

So, I went to visit the one person who could cheer me up.

"Sweetheart, you've been holding the same puzzle piece for

the last ten minutes." Grams nods at the blue-and-gold tile in my hand.

"Hmm?" I reply, not fully processing her comment.

She gives me a soft smile, plucking the piece from my hand and fitting it into place on the card table. The replica of Van Gogh's *Starry Night* is now more than halfway complete, no thanks to me.

I run my fingers through my hair, glancing out the window. "I'm sorry, I've been a little distracted."

Grams chuckles. "A little? Sweetheart, earlier you put the TV remote in my mini fridge, agreed to stop drinking pumpkin spice lattes when I suggested you should cut back on your caffeine intake, and now this—" She waves a hand at the puzzle. "Not to mention you came to visit at three o'clock on a Friday afternoon, when you're usually at work."

"Dawson told me to take the rest of the day off," I answer vaguely.

"Is everything okay?" She carefully slides the card table to the side and turns to face me. "That's the first time you've mentioned Dawson since you've been here and you look like you're on the verge of tears." She takes my hand in hers, running her finger along my palm in soothing strokes.

Dawson has come with me to visit Grams several times, and she's quickly become as smitten with him as I am. It's no surprise that he's a big hit with all the ladies at bingo night.

"I'm sort of out of a job, at least until next week. Dawson is leaving the firm to start his own," I add, noticing the furrow in her brow. "And he's asked me to go with him."

Dawson has the power and influence to make it a successful venture, but that doesn't mean it's any less daunting to think about. I was just getting settled at Thompson & Tate, and now he wants me to start over at a new firm, when our relationship is still so new.

"It sounds like a great opportunity," Grams remarks.

"He also asked me to move in with him," I say.

Her expression brightens and she clasps her hands together. "Oh, that's wonderful, sweetheart. Why aren't we celebrating?"

I should have figured this would be her reaction. "Grams, he asked me to *move in* with him," I say, placing my hand on her arm. "As in, live together under the same roof for an undetermined amount of time. We haven't really known each other very long."

"So what?" She shrugs. "There are no rules to suggest a definitive timeline when you've found the right person. Your grandfather and I took it one step further and got married a month after we met. That turned out to be the best decision we ever made," she says with a fond smile.

My eyebrows shoot up in surprise. "How come you never told me?"

Growing up they shared countless stories about their life as a married couple, but now that I think about it, they seldom talked about their time together before they tied the knot. At least now I know why.

"Because it was irrelevant. What mattered most were the forty years of memories we created together." Grams pauses, her gaze shifting to a wedding photo of her and Grandpa framed on the bureau. "Is there a reason Dawson wants you to move in so soon? For your grandfather, it was because he didn't want to spend a single night apart."

I look away, releasing a slow, deep breath. "Dawson came to the house a few weeks ago, and when he saw its condition, he insisted that I stay with him. It's been absolutely wonderful, but I'm worried that we're moving too fast."

Grams furrows her brows. "What's the condition of the house?" she urges when I don't immediately offer additional details.

Overcome with shame, my lips tremble. I had hoped to have a solution in place before admitting to Grams the severity of the situation with the house, but it looks like my time is up.

"I haven't been able to keep the house maintained," I admit, my face burning with embarrassment. "The furnace isn't working, the floors in your room are rotting, there's a minor mold problem in the spare bedroom… and that's just the tip of the iceberg. I can't afford to fix it all, not with all the other expenses coming in." I avert my gaze, afraid of seeing her reaction.

Grams let out a small gasp, clutching my hand tighter. "Oh, Reese. Why didn't you tell me?" she asks, her tone despondent.

"I'm sorry, Grams," I murmur. "I was afraid of letting you down. You trusted me to take care of the house, and I failed." I stare down at the floor, struggling to keep the tears at bay.

She places her hand on my cheek, encouraging me to look at her. "Oh, sweet girl. It breaks my heart that you've been dealing with this alone." Grams speaks softly, tears glistening in her own eyes. It seems we're both struggling to keep our emotions at bay. "It's my fault for not telling you to sell it sooner."

I chew on my lower lip as I consider what she's suggesting. "But it means so much to you. How can you even think about giving it up?"

It was her home for over forty years, the place where she spent the most time with both my mom and grandpa.

"All the memories I cherish most are right here." Grams taps her temple, a warm smile spreading across her face. "Your happiness means more than the house ever did. In the past, we've had several developers interested in the property and I'm sure they're still interested. Selling it should leave you with a substantial profit."

"The money isn't important." I press my lips together. "You really think I should sell?" I finally ask.

"I want you to do what will make you happy," she corrects me. "It's time to turn the page, Reese. You've got a promising future ahead and that should be your focus." Her eyes shine with warmth.

My mind spins as Grams words sink in. I never entertained the idea of giving up the house since it didn't seem like an option before. Truth be told, I let my fear of failing her cloud my judgment and never asked her directly. Instead, keeping my focus on finding ways to afford to maintain the house since I assumed she wanted me to keep it. Now that I'm faced with the possibility of letting go and starting a new chapter, I'm left with a sense of uncertainty.

"What if I move in with Dawson and things don't work out?" I ask, voicing my concern.

"You'll have a good cry, then you'll come here to play bingo, watch back-to-back episodes of your favorite shows, and find solace in the bottom of an ice cream tub. After that we'll find you a stunning apartment with a beautiful view of the skyline." She taps her finger on her mouth, hinting that she has more to share. "But what if moving in with him *does* work out?" Gram pauses to give me a chance to think about it. "If it were me, I'd rather take the risk then play it safe and always wonder if I missed out on something incredible."

She has always been my greatest cheerleader, her support unwavering. I wouldn't be where I am today without her. Though I wish I could have had more time with my mom, I'll forever cherish the close relationship I have with Grams.

I get up to give her a big hug. "I love you so much."

"I love you too, Reese."

She swipes a stray tear from my face with her thumb and wipes it on the blanket draped over her lap. I furrow my brow, wondering how I hadn't noticed it before. It looks new so I assume she won it in another round of bingo or one of her friends gave it to her.

With my mind cleared now, I help Grams finish the puzzle, and then we say our goodbyes.

On my way out of the facility, April waves me down near the reception desk. She must have started her shift after I got here.

"Reese, did you hear what happened?" she asks as she sets out new flyers advertising a knitting class for the residences.

"I haven't," I admit, glancing around the reception area, hoping for some clue as to what she's referring to.

She leans over the desk, her voice dropping to a whisper. "A generous donor donated ten million dollars to the facility, enough to cover all the residents' care for a full year." She claps her hands, her voice filled with excitement. "You should get a call from the administrator soon, but I couldn't let you leave without telling you the wonderful news."

My expression goes slack. "Do you know who it was?"

She shakes her head. "They asked to remain anonymous."

"Do you happen to know if the same donor had new blankets delivered to the residents?"

April chuckles. "Actually, yes. They told the administrator to get two cashmere blankets for every resident. It's a sweet gesture since it tends to get cold here at night," she says as she tightens her sweater around her middle.

"Thanks so much for letting me know," I say on my way out.

I think back to the night Dawson came to bingo with us and Grams shared how she's always wanted a cashmere blanket. This grand gesture has to be him. There's no one else with that kind of money who would do something this thoughtful for this specific facility.

With my mind still reeling on what my next steps are, I need a little more time to process, so I head back to my house. When I arrive, there's a bouquet of two dozen sunflowers on the porch accompanied by a simple note.

I had the furnace fixed – D

When I left the office, I didn't tell him where I was going. Yet, he somehow knew I'd come back here eventually. My pulse is racing as I fiddle with my keys, and I'm enveloped in warmth when I finally step inside the house. However, aside from the heat now working, it's the same as when I left.

Reese: Thank you for the flowers and for fixing the furnace.

Dawson: I couldn't let you go back to a cold house.

Dawson: I'm glad you made it home safe.

Strange how this place doesn't quite feel like home anymore.

Reese: Are you still at the office?

Dawson: I'm at Steel & Ink. I just finished an angel tattoo and it made me think of you.

The sentiment makes butterflies dance in my stomach.

As I survey the rundown living room, a thought occurs to me. Dawson could have easily had the place renovated while I've been staying with him, but he didn't. While he's not afraid to cross most boundaries, he somehow knew that I needed to make this particular decision on my own, and I appreciate it more than I can say.

Grams was right—this place is just a house. A home isn't defined by a structure with four walls or an address. It's the feeling of belonging. It's unconditional love. And now I understand that my home is where my heart is—with Dawson.

CHAPTER 21

Dawson

AFTER PACKING UP MY OFFICE, AND MAKING COUNTLESS calls to clients, I was ready to leave for the last time. Coming to the tattoo shop tonight was a good distraction. My first client served in the military, and a few years ago his fellow service member died in the line of duty. He wanted his dog tags tattooed on his arm as a tribute to their friendship. My second client is one year sober, and celebrated by getting a guardian angel tattoo on her shoulder.

It's now past closing, and Mickey and the rest of the staff left an hour ago.

I'm wiping down the reception desk when my phone rings. I frown when I see Martha's name on the screen, wishing it was Reese since she didn't text me back after asking where I was, and I had hoped she would stop by or at least call me so we could still talk tonight.

"Hi Martha," I answer.

"Hey, honey. How are you?" she asks.

"We haven't heard from you in a few days and wanted to check in," Colby chimes in.

I toss the cloth I was using to clean into the trash. "Yeah, I'm sorry, things have been busy at the office." I start pacing the floor, raking my hand through my hair. "I actually quit today to start a new firm."

Since I started working at Thompson & Tate, Colby was skeptical. Still, he has consistently offered his encouragement. Even after learning about Maxwell's embezzlement, he encouraged me every step of the way when I dug the firm out of the hole Maxwell put us in.

So, I shouldn't be surprised when he says, "It's about damn time."

"You don't think it's a reckless idea?"

"Was it an impulsive decision?" Colby questions.

I scoff. "No, of course not. I'd been preparing for his confrontation for a while now. I'm taking most of my clients and team with me, and I've made sure there's nothing Maxwell can do to stop me," I state proudly. "I also spoke to my realtor this afternoon, and we found the perfect office with a view of Central Park."

"There's your answer, son. Martha and I couldn't be more proud of you."

"That's right. We're so happy for you, honey," Martha adds.

A sense of warmth spreads through my chest at hearing their unwavering support. This next chapter in my life will be challenging, but having Martha and Colby in my corner will make it easier.

I can't help but think of Reese. More than anything, I want her by my side for whatever comes next.

"How's Reese holding up?" Martha asks when I don't reply. "She's going to work with you at the new firm right?" I can almost hear the satisfaction in her voice.

"I hope so," I say, keeping my reply vague.

There's a brief silence on the other end of the phone before

Martha speaks. "Dawson Cole Tate, what did you do?" She accuses me.

I'd like to refute any wrongdoing but I can't deny that her motherly instincts are spot on.

I rub the back of my neck as I pace the floor. "I didn't tell Reese about my plan to quit and start a new firm until after things were finalized with Maxwell," I admit hesitantly.

"That's not all is it?" Martha presses, like she can sense there's more to the story.

"I might have asked her to move in with me during the same conversation. She's living in the house she inherited from her grandparents, but it's falling apart around her. I just want her to be safe and more importantly with me."

"Oh, Dawson," Martha sighs, her tone tinged with disappointment. "I know you're used to having things your way, but a healthy relationship means including your partner in the decision-making process."

"Martha's right," Colby interjects. "Communication is key, and the primary reason we've stayed together. Her opinion matters more to me than anything else, and I always want to know what she thinks before making a decision, especially when it directly affects her."

"You're incredibly driven, but sometimes you jump into situations without considering the impact on those around you. Put yourself in Reese's shoes. You've just started seeing each other, and in a single day, you've not only upheaved her job, but are asking her to upend her life by moving in with you." Martha pauses, giving a moment for her words to settle. "I'm glad that you know what you want, but it's important to consider Reese's needs. Otherwise, you risk pushing her away."

When Martha puts it that way Reese's reaction at the office earlier makes more sense.

Control has been one of my coping mechanisms for as long as

I can remember. Now, I'm beginning to understand that being in a relationship means I have to be willing to compromise if I want to make things work with Reese, even if it's against my instincts.

I consider what Martha said about seeing things from Reese's perspective. I wouldn't have been so polite about having my job upended and being asked a life-changing question without having time to process it.

The last thing I want is to risk losing Reese because of my inability to compromise and give her what she deserves: an equal say in our future.

"You're right, Martha, I have to..." I trail off when the chime of the bell on the front door rings.

Dammit. I must have forgotten to lock up.

My expression darkens, ready to unleash on whoever it is, but I stop in my tracks when I see Reese standing in the doorway. Her red hair spills down her shoulders, and her emerald eyes are fixed on me. My gaze moves down her body, a soft smile passes my lips when I notice she's wearing her white sneakers with sunflowers drawn on the sides.

"Dawson, are you still there? Is everything okay? Martha asks over the phone.

"Reese is here. Can I call you tomorrow?"

"Yes, of course. Just make things right so we can meet her soon," Martha says, her tone tinged with hope.

"Sweetheart, he'll be fine," Colby interjects. "We'll talk to you later Dawson," he says before hanging up.

I tuck my phone in my pocket, never taking my eyes off Reese.

"Hi," she offers with a small wave.

"You're here," I say, stunned.

"I am."

When she didn't text back earlier, part of me was worried she had decided to end things but didn't know how to tell me. Now I'm worried that she's going to do it in person.

I've made up my mind that if that's the case, I'm going to do everything in my power to change her mind. Because seeing her here solidifies that she belongs to me. There's nothing more important, and I'm prepared to put everything on the line if that's what it takes to keep her in my life.

"What are you doing here?" I ask cautiously.

She takes a deep breath as she glances around the shop. "I'd like to get a tattoo," she states confidently. "That is if you're still open." She gestures around the empty tattoo parlor.

I stare at her shocked—those were the last words I expected to hear.

It takes me back to the first night she was here. Her bubbly personality and natural charm were a breath of fresh air from my mundane existence. So much has changed since then, but the one thing that remains the same is the unrelenting need to draw her close.

"Really?" I ask.

"Yes." She strides toward me. "Someone once told me tattoos that have a personal meaning are the best kind. I've thought long and hard about it, and I want one right here." She motions to her wrist.

"What tattoo were you thinking?"

"A compass, similar to this one." She reaches out to trace mine with the tip of her finger. "But smaller so it fits on my wrist, with sunflowers around it."

I nod, the design already taking shape in my mind. "Follow me," I say, guiding her to my station. Once we're inside, she takes a seat in the tattoo chair and places her wrist face up on the armrest. She silently watches me as I gather my supplies, she winces when I wipe her wrist with a cold antiseptic wipe.

"You sure about this, Red? Getting a tattoo can be painful,

especially here," I lightly touch her wrist. "The skin is thin, and the nerves are more sensitive."

She nods with a smile. "I'm positive."

I retrieve a black surgical marker and crouch down on my stool, bending over Reese's arm to draw. Most tattoo artists use tablets to create their designs, however I prefer drawing freehand on the skin as it gives me more creative freedom.

With slow, consistent strokes, I begin to outline the compass.

"Why this particular design?" I inquire, unable to hide my curiosity.

"Sunflowers were my grandpa's favorite flower," Reese says, her tone carrying a hint of longing. "When my mom got sick, she planted a handful of sunflower seeds in the backyard, but they didn't sprout. One of my first memories was the following year when I woke up on a Saturday morning to find both my grandparents looking out the back window with tears in their eyes. My grandpa held me up so I could see the beautiful cluster of sunflowers that had bloomed, and told me it was a sign that my mom was watching over us." I pause to glance up to find Reese has tears gleaming in her eyes. "The sunflowers are a way to keep their memory alive," she adds softly, her voice cracking slightly.

"It's a beautiful tribute, Red. I'll do my best to honor their memory." I lean forward to place a chaste kiss to her temple. "Thank you for trusting me to do this."

Reese wipes away a stray tear with her free hand. "There's no one else I'd rather share this moment with. I know you'll create something special." She rests her head as I return to outlining the tattoo. "The compass is for me," she whispers a few seconds later. "A reminder to trust myself to navigate through life's challenges and stay true to my own path. There's also someone very important in my life who has a similar one and I like the idea of wearing a symbol that has significance for both of us."

I briefly glance up from my work again. "He feels the same

way," I murmur, swallowing the lump in my throat, forcing my attention to the design taking shape on Reese's wrist—the vintage compass has four cardinal points, encircled by a ring of sunflowers, the petals wrapping around the curve of her wrist. Once I finish outlining, I prepare the tattoo gun, and Reese squeezes her eyes shut, tensing up when the needle pierces her skin for the first time.

I hesitate, worry etched on my face. "Should I stop?"

"No. It stings, but I can handle it." She gives me a confident grin, trying to mask the discomfort with a brave front.

I've tattooed hundreds of clients, but watching her suffer the slightest bit of discomfort makes me second-guess every stroke of the needle. What drives me forward is knowing this tattoo is important to her, and the trust she's placed in me to get it right.

The rhythmic buzz of the tattoo machine creates a steady hum as I stay focused on making sure each line is precise. It's difficult since I'm hyper-aware of every shift in Reese' posture, and each soft exhale when I shift the needle's position. When my gloved hand brushes against her skin, it sends an electric current rippling through me. Even the thin material can't stop the visceral reaction I have to her. After what feels like hours, I finally finish, and when her emerald eyes shift to mine, the weight of our unspoken feelings hangs in the air.

I gently clean the area with another antiseptic wipe, and apply a layer of ointment to protect her new ink. Reese's gaze moves to her wrist, a smile brightening her face. "It's perfect, Dawson," she says in awe.

"I'm glad you think so." I carefully wrap the tattoo, her pulse quickening with every touch.

My fingers linger, and I can't help lifting her hand to my mouth, placing a tender kiss below the area that's covered by the protective wrap.

"I spent the afternoon with Grams." Reese speaks up. "She told me I should sell the house."

"Are you going to?" I ask hesitantly.

"Yes, I think I am." She says, her fingers twitching in my hold.

A part of me is relieved that Georgia suggested Reese sell. Whether she chooses to move in with me or find her own place, I'm glad she'll no longer be living in an unsafe environment. Still, I recognize this must be a difficult decision to leave the home she's lived in her whole life.

I give her hand a gentle squeeze. "I'm here for whatever you need."

She chews on her lower lip, her gaze locked on mine. "There is one thing."

"Which is?" I press when she doesn't continue.

"I'm going to need a place to stay."

"Is this your way of telling me you want to move in with me, Red?" I grin, my excitement barely contained.

"If the offer still stands," she says hesitantly.

I motion for her to stand, guiding her by the hand to sit on my lap. When she's seated, I wind my hand around her waist, nuzzling my nose into her neck.

"It does," I assure her. "But if you're unsure we can wait to take that step."

My conversation with Martha & Colby made me see that as long as I have Reese in my life, everything else will fall into place in its own time.

Reese shakes her head. "There's nowhere else I'd rather be than with you," she states.

"But I'm paying rent. I don't want a free ride, even if you're my boyfriend."

"*Boyfriend*, huh? I like the sound of that."

There's no way I'm letting her pay rent, but we can figure out a way for her to contribute if that'll make her happy.

She runs her fingers through my hair as she snuggles closer. "Something interesting happened at Oak Ridge today—two things actually. Grams had a new cashmere blanket that she kept on her lap the whole time I was there, and on the way out, April, one of the receptionists told me that an anonymous donor paid for all the residents' fees for a year. You wouldn't happen to know anything about that now, would you?"

I give her a wry smile. "That's incredibly generous." I say, sidestepping her question. "I'd wager the person who did it must care a lot about someone who lives there. In fact, I'd go as far to say they must love someone related to that resident... her granddaughter maybe?"

Reese sits up in my lap, blinking in shock. "Dawson?" she utters, hesitating as if afraid to voice her question.

I graze my knuckles across her jawline, my gaze meeting hers. "I love you, Reese Taylor." I state with conviction. "I love you so damn much, and I can't imagine a life without you in it."

She places her hand over mine, keeping it pressed to her cheek. "I love you too, Dawson, and now that we're together, I'm never letting you go."

"Never," I vow.

CHAPTER 22

Reese

THREE MONTHS LATER

I SAUNTER INTO DAWSON'S OFFICE, LOCKING THE DOOR behind me.

His new firm is in a high-rise overlooking Central Park and the city skyline.

This morning, he finally settled the Irving case, and I got to witness firsthand as he got justice for his client—Wes Irving. Wes had launched a startup for an AI-powered financial app, but lost ownership after bringing on additional investors which diluted his control of the business and reduced his profit share. With Dawson's help, Wes has bought back his original stake in the company and has been reinstated as the CEO.

Watching Dawson in action this morning was a form of foreplay I didn't know existed. It was hot as hell witnessing him command that room and make grown men cower. I almost lost it when he rolled up his shirt sleeves, exposing his tattooed forearms.

For so long, he's kept his tattoos concealed, thinking he had to fit a certain image or his reputation would be tarnished.

However, it seems like he's now accepted they're part of who he is. The ink on his arms is irrelevant to clients when he delivers the results they expect, and they add an extra edge to the intimidation factor when he needs to use it.

Plus they're sexy as hell.

The last three months have been especially hectic for us both.

Dawson's had to balance starting the new firm, juggling endless meetings, and tight deadlines. Yet, through it all, he never fails to find time for me.

In addition to settling into the new firm, I've recently experienced several significant changes in my life.

Noah and I took the LSAT four weeks ago and got our results yesterday.

We both scored in the one-seventies, which should be sufficient for admission to a top law school in New York. However, I'm open to accepting any offers to law schools in the area, as long as I can commute from Brooklyn and have enough time to visit Grams each week.

Now that we don't have to study anymore, Noah and I meet up for weekend brunch instead. He's still going strong with David, and I'm so glad he's found someone who makes him happy.

Last month, the sale of Grams' house was finalized. We sold it to a developer who owns the neighboring lots. They plan to turn the area into a new apartment complex for low-income families.

Saying goodbye to the house was bitter-sweet, but Grams and I spent hours going through keepsakes, reminiscing about the memories tied to each one. Knowing that Grams is at peace with the decision is the closure I needed to fully let go.

Dawson is seated at his desk, engaged in an animated call with opposing counsel for another case. A workaholic by nature, he never turns down a high-stakes case, no matter how much is on his plate.

"No, my client won't accept those terms," he growls. His tone is gruff, and whoever is on the other end gets an earful.

He left the apartment earlier than usual this morning to prepare for the Irving meeting, so he missed our morning ritual, which usually includes him inside me, his face buried between my legs or my mouth wrapped around his cock.

Moving in with him has been one of the best decisions I've ever made. We compromised on me paying for groceries and take-out when we're not in the mood to cook. I tried offering to contribute to other expenses, but he insisted on covering the rest.

When I tried to protest, he explained that he wanted me to set up an investment plan to manage the proceeds Grams and I received from selling the house. That way, one day, I could use the funds to start a nonprofit or my own firm dedicated to advocating for children's rights after I graduate.

There was no way I could argue with that.

Dawson is generous, thoughtful and loves me unconditionally. On occasion his bossy side comes out, but my stubbornness always balances us out.

A smile plays on my lips as I approach his desk, dropping to my knees in front of him.

His gaze sears into me as he mutes his call. "Red, what are you doing?" His voice is strained.

I bat my eyelashes. "Taking care of my boss. You've had such a stressful morning Mr. Tate, and I want to help you take the edge off." I answer in a sultry tone.

Dawson strokes my head, and I lean into his touch. "You're such a good girl."

His words of praise have me nuzzling into this touch. The fact that we're in his office in the middle of the day is pushed aside; the driving need to taste him overriding everything else.

Dawson opens his legs in silent invitation, and I scoot closer to unbuckle his belt and unfasten his slacks. He sits perfectly still as I pull down his zipper.

He unmutes his call. "Yes, I'm here," he snaps to the person on the phone.

I lift my hooded eyes to meet his smoldering gaze as I curl my fingers around his thick cock. He inhales sharply as I move my hand up and down his shaft in slow, steady strokes. Pre-cum leaks from the tip, and I lean forward to lap it up with my tongue.

"No, my client wants five million, that's nonnegotiable."

Dawson wraps his fist around my ponytail, guiding himself into my mouth. I greedily accept, sucking the crown with fervor, and when he tightens his grip, coaxing me to take him deeper, I hollow out my cheeks until his head is at the back of my throat. He lets me set the pace as I adjust.

He covers the phone with his hand. "Such a naughty girl," he groans as he strokes the column of my neck.

My panties are completely soaked through, his praise fueling my desire. I cup his balls, squeezing gently, as I suck him off.

"The answer is no, Carl. Call me back when you have a better offer." He hangs up and tosses his phone on the desk.

"Fuck, Red, you're a goddamn vision with your mouth around my cock."

I hum around his length in reply.

Dawson loses all control, tugging my head forward as he moves me at the pace he wants. He lets out a growl of approval as I suck him with fervor, eager to please.

I'm drunk on the knowledge that I'm the reason for his unrestrained pleasure. I grip his thighs, clawing at his pants as my mouth bobs up and down on his shaft.

"I'm going to come," he groans.

He gently tugs my hair to pull me off but I ignore him, and suck harder. His cock jerks under my hand as his cum fills my mouth. His eyes widen as I lap up every drop, licking him clean.

When I'm finished, his cock springs free from my mouth with a loud pop.

Dawson extends a hand to help me up and lifts me onto his desk, shoving aside several stacks of paperwork to make room. He grips my jaw, pulling me in for a searing kiss. His presence is all-consuming as he towers over me, gazing down with those piercing blue eyes I love so much.

He nips my ear. "I'm going to fuck you now, angel."

"Yes." I breathe out the single word as a shiver ripples down my spine.

I need Dawson like I need my next breath, and I'm at his mercy, addicted to his touch. He hikes my skirt up over my hips and yanks my panties to the side, stepping between my legs while grabbing hold of his still-hard cock.

"And you thought I was old," he taunts as he pushes inside me in one deep thrust.

"Oh, fuck, Dawson," I cry out.

He slants his mouth across mine to swallow my moans as he as his thrusts work up to almost a punishing pace. I wrap my hands around his neck, tangling my fingers in his hair, savoring the feel of being so full. He lifts up on the balls of his feet, giving himself the extra height he needs to plunge in deeper, allowing me to feel every single inch of him. He drops his head against my shoulder, putting all his energy into driving home.

He reaches down and alternates between flicking and rolling my clit with his thumb and forefinger, and soon we're both bar-reling toward our release.

"You're taking me so well, Red. This pussy was made for me," he murmurs as he plants a soft kiss against my nose. "I can't wait until we get home tonight so I can take my time with you."

"Looking forward to it," I say with a sated smile.

Being with Dawson has brought me more happiness than I ever imagined. I'll be forever grateful to the universe for bringing us together and for that fateful day I stumbled into his tattoo shop, which led us here.

He's proven that there is such a thing as a fairytale ending, complete with grand gestures and a love that surpasses all hopes. Except in place of a prince and a carriage, my happily-ever-after comes with a sexy, tatted lawyer, one where I ride off into the sunset on the back of his bike.

Getting a new boss didn't turn out anything like I expected, but now I know what happens when you give a lawyer a kiss...

He becomes my home, the place where my heart belongs.

EPILOGUE

Dawson

TIME HAS FLOWN BY SINCE STARTING THE FIRM, AND WELL, Reese has kept me busy.

The new law office is named Tate & Larsen. I brought on a second managing partner, Mark Larsen. We met in law school, and I trust him to bring valuable insights and leadership to the team. It helps that he's not afraid to bend the rules when necessary to achieve the best outcomes for our clients. And having him on board has lightened my workload, allowing me more time for other priorities.

The majority of the attorneys and support staff from Maxwell's firm came to work for me, including Reese's friend Grace. Now, they work on the same floor, and go to lunch together at least once a week.

Reese is Mark's paralegal, and although I still miss having her report directly to me, she's only down the hall and visits my office. Frequently.

Occasionally for official business, but more often than not, I spend our time together between her legs.

Every Saturday night, Reese and I go to the tattoo shop. She's designed several floral tattoos that have become popular with my clients and while I ink them, she helps Mickey and the rest of the staff with other tasks. After we finish up at the shop, I always take her to Tuscany Table. The mushroom risotto is now Reese's favorite. It's the one day a week we have to ourselves, and can disconnect from the pressures of the firm and our other responsibilities.

Going home together is the best part of the day. Our house smells like coconut and pineapple, there's usually at least one pair of sneakers left in the hallway and an abundance of throw pillows decorating the bed and couch, thanks to Martha taking Reese shopping whenever she and Colby come into town.

They're absolutely smitten with Reese, and this year, we're planning to host Thanksgiving at the brownstone with Grams, Martha, Colby, Christian, and Seren in attendance. We're hoping to make it a tradition to have everyone we love gathered together to recognize everything we're grateful for. Since Reese came into my life, it's become a long list.

Today might not be a holiday, but we have a lot to celebrate.

"Dawson, Reese, what a delightful surprise." Georgia beams, setting her book aside on the windowsill. "I wasn't expecting to see you again until tomorrow."

We visit her at Oak Ridge every week, and never miss bingo night. On Sundays, she spends the day at our place, and Grams likes to brag to Ms. Werther that this past summer she got to work on her tan while lounging by the rooftop pool with Reese and Noah.

"Reese couldn't wait until tomorrow to share the news," I say with a smirk.

If she hadn't been distracted this morning—splayed out on the kitchen counter with my head between her thighs she would have insisted we come sooner. As it is, I couldn't resist taking the opportunity to enjoy a few moments alone with her.

Georgia's worried gaze pings between Reese and me. "Is something wrong?"

Reese pulls up a chair next to Grams, offering her a reassuring smile. "There's no need to worry. It's all good news, I promise."

"Well? What is it?" Grams asks, not concealing her impatience as she leans forward in her chair.

Reese pauses a beat to build anticipation, a broad smile lighting her face. "I was accepted into law school," she announces, practically bouncing in her seat. "I start in the fall."

"Oh, sweetheart," Georgia exclaims with tears in her eyes. "That's the most wonderful news. I'm so proud of you." She squeezes Reese's hand. "I wish your mom and grandfather could be here to celebrate." She wipes away a tear that has slipped down her cheek.

"Me too, Grams," Reese says somberly. "But I'm so grateful you're here. None of this would have been possible without you."

"Hush now," Grams waves her off. "I can't wait to hear all about your classes once you start." When Reese and I remain silent, Georgia casts a glance my way, a flash of confusion on her face. "You said *it's all good news.* Do you have anything else to tell me?"

Reese tilts her head, brushing a piece of hair from her face. "Like what?"

"Oh, nothing. I'm just an old woman wishing that one of these days you'll have another life-changing announcement to share that involves a diamond ring."

I purse my lips to keep from smirking.

For the past year, she's been not so discreetly hinting that Reese and I should get married. The day Reese told her we were officially dating, the first question she asked was, "When's the wedding." The woman is relentless. And while she'll have to wait a while longer for the wedding itself, she might be interested in what Reese has to say next.

"You mean like this diamond?" Reese asks, holding out her left hand.

She's slipped on the custom engagement ring I gave her this morning. The band is made with a cluster of stones forming petals around a four-carat oval-shaped diamond. It's as unique as the woman who's wearing it.

"Oh, I can't believe it," Georgia exclaims as he pulls Reese's hand closer to get a better look. "It's beautiful." She leans forward to kiss Reese on the cheek, before doing the same to me. "I love you both so much."

"We love you too, Grams," Reese says with a smile.

My thoughts wander back to earlier today when I asked Reese the most important question I've ever asked up to this point in my life.

"Dawson, where are you?" Reese shouts from the bedroom.

"I'm in the kitchen," I holler as I pour a fresh cup of coffee and add a heavy dose of pumpkin spice creamer just the way she likes it.

I hear her footsteps echo down the hall, and a moment later, she bursts through the doorway with a wide grin.

"I did it," she exclaims. "I got in."

Reese holds out her phone to show me the acceptance letter. It's official. She'll be starting law school in New York City this fall. During the application process, she refused to let me use my connections to put in a good word for her. She wanted to get in on her own merit, and I couldn't be more proud of her.

She'll be quitting the firm once she starts law school, and although it'll take some getting used to not having her around the office, I'm excited for her to achieve her dreams. I'll be there every step of the way cheering her on, and making sure she has plenty of pumpkin spice lattes at her disposal. One of the perks of having unlimited resources is I'm able to get her favorite specialty creamer year-round.

"You did it, Red." I wrap my arms around her waist and spin us in a circle, her melodic laugh fills the air, making my heart swell with

happiness. These little moments are the ones I cherish most with her. When it's just the two of us, in our private bubble where every laugh and smile is a precious gift, and the outside world fades away. "Did you talk to Noah yet?" I ask.

Reese nods. "He texted me a few minutes ago to say he got his acceptance letter, too," she exclaims.

They both applied to the same law schools, so it's a relief they got into the one at the top of their list. I'm glad Reese will have his support not only as a friend but as a reliable study partner too.

"I love you so damn much," I say, molding my mouth to hers.

"Mmm," she murmurs against my lips. "I love you too, Dawson."

As much as I want to hoist her up on the counter and have my way with her, there's an important question I have to ask first.

Reese grumbles when I pull back, blinking up at me with curiosity.

I reach into my pocket to retrieve the custom engagement ring I picked up from the jeweler last night. While I agreed to stay out of the law school application process, I may have pulled some strings to get a heads up when acceptance letters went out and to confirm Reese was on that list. I wanted to time this perfectly, and it seemed like the ideal opportunity to make an already perfect day even more special.

I drop to one knee and look up at Reese.

"Dawson, what are you doing?" she whispers.

"I know you want to hold off on getting married until after you graduate, and I can live with that. However, I can't wait that long to ask you to be mine." I clear my throat, keeping my gaze locked on emerald eyes, sparking with anticipation. "If I were to list out all the reasons I wanted to spend the rest of my life with you, I'd run out of breath before I finished. So instead, I'll make you this simple promise: Our life together will be filled with love, adventure, and happiness. And every morning, I'll wake up thankful to have you by my side and to call you mine."

I take her hand, tracing my fingertips along her knuckles before sliding the engagement ring onto her index finger.

"Aren't you supposed to ask me a question first?" Reese asks, her lips curving into a teasing smile, while she admires the ring.

"Reese Taylor, make me the happiest man alive and say you'll marry me?"

She beams as she nods rapidly. "Yes. Absolutely yes."

I stand up, and tug her into my embrace, basking in the knowledge that the person I get to spend the rest of my life with is right in front of me.

We've made several compromises along the way, from her moving in and my agreement to wait to get married until she graduates law school. The ring on her finger means I can be a little more patient while she chases her dreams. For now, having her in my bed every night and her clothes taking over half my closet is more than enough. They're signs of the life we're building together, and now that she's agreed to be mine, I'm never letting her go.

When I get to the bar, Harrison is at the far end, glaring at his Old Fashioned like it's offended him somehow. It's been a few weeks since we've met up. Every spare moment outside of the new firm is dedicated to Reese. She's with Noah and his boyfriend David, watching a Hallmark movie marathon tonight. It's their way of celebrating our engagement and their acceptance into law school. I'd do anything for her, but I was relieved when she suggested I grab a drink with Harrison instead.

I slide into the seat next to Harrison. "Now a bad time to cash in my second favor?" I tease.

He'll be waiting a while for me to collect it. I have something in mind but it has to wait until Reese has graduated law school, no matter how much I want to do it sooner.

Harrison glances over, his expression flat. "I'm not in the mood for your antics today."

"You're gloomier than usual," I observe. "Want to talk about it, *friend*?"

"Nope."

I nod at the bartender when he slides over two fingers of brandy. I'm mid-sip when Harrison's phone rings, and he groans before answering.

"Yes, Fallon?" He asks tersely.

His eyes widen and he slams his fist against the bar. "I swear to god, woman, if you break my hockey stick there will be hell to pay." Yelling erupts on the other end and his jaw tightens as he holds the phone away from his ear.

"How was I supposed to know it was so damn expensive? It smelled bad so I tossed it out." Harrison rakes his hand through his hair while listening to Fallon's response.

"My aversion to fish isn't the issue, and no, I'm out with a friend, and won't be back until late." He frowns when there's no response. "Hello? Fallon, are you there?" He tosses the phone on the counter, and downs his drink in one gulp. "I can't believe she hung up on me," he mutters to himself.

I interrupt his pity party with a smirk. "Is hockey stick a euphemism?"

"If only," he mutters. "Fallon's on a rampage because I threw out a Bluefin Tuna that supposedly was worth two hundred grand. She says a client got it from an auction in Japan and sent it to her as a thank you gift." He rolls his eyes. "How the hell was I supposed to know something that smells so bad could cost as much as a sports car?"

Their heated exchange the night at the club hinted at some unresolved tension between them, which was only unscored by him ignoring her call when Reese and I were in the car with him in Aspen Grove. This begs the question of why Fallon is at his house?

I glance at my watch. "Why is she at your place at 10:00 pm, and more importantly, why is she keeping her fish in your fridge? I thought you didn't like her."

He grits his teeth. "Because my mom can't help herself from meddling in my business, and suggested Fallon stay with me." He grunts, not offering any more details.

I clap him on the back, chuckling. "Good luck, man; sounds like you'll need it."

While he's dreading going home, I'm looking forward to it— anxious to get back to Reese.

As a kid I never thought I'd be lucky enough to have a family and now I'm surrounded by supportive parents and a fiancé who brings out the best in me, proving that love really does exist.

Want to see the surprise Dawson has up his sleeve when Reese graduates from law school? Type this link into your browser to read the extended epilogue for *When You Give a Lawyer a Kiss*:

https://dl.bookfunnel.com/vnia2lj564

Thank you for taking the time to read *When You Give a Lawyer a Kiss*. If you enjoyed this book, please consider leaving a review on your preferred platform(s) of choice. It's the best compliment I can receive as an author, and it makes it easier for other readers to find my books.

OTHER BOOKS BY ANN EINERSON

If You Give a Grump a Holiday Wishlist (Presley & Jack)
*A small town, fake dating, one bed spicy workplace
holiday romance.*

If You Give a Single Dad a Nanny (Dylan & Marlow)
*A swoon worthy, single dad/nanny, age gap, he's grumpy, she's
sunshine, banter-filled spicy small town romance*

If You Give a Billionaire a Bride (Cash & Everly)
*A marriage of convenience that starts with a Vegas wedding
between a reformed playboy and his best friend's sister in a banter-
filled spicy billionaire romance*

The Spotlight (Conway & Sienna)
*A best friend's brother, opposites attract, dating in secret,
spicy rockstar romance.*

ACKNOWLEDGMENTS

There are so many people who made this book possible, and I can't thank you all enough for your love, kindness, and support. When You Give a Lawyer a Kiss wouldn't have been possible without each and every one of you.

To Bryanna—For being the best co-worker and collaborator. You make the day-to-day of being a writer so much more fun and far less lonely, and am grateful for your friendship always.

To Autumn—I'm so lucky our paths crossed. Thanks for your blunt honesty when I need to hear it and your dedication to helping me achieve my goals. I couldn't do this without you.

To Tab and Kaity—Words cannot adequately express my gratitude for you. Thank you for putting up with my endless DMs, questions, and concerns. Your feedback is invaluable and this story would never have made it down on paper without you cheering me on from the sidelines.

To Jess, Kenz, and Madison—Thank you for helping to spread the word about When You Give a Lawyer a Kiss and for your creative input. Your ability to bring my vision to life always amazes me and I'm so incredibly grateful to work alongside each of you.

To Nicole, Lyndsey and Britt—I couldn't have asked for a better editing team. I'm grateful for your expertise and for pushing me to write a story worth reading.

To Caroline, Wren, Lauren Brooke, Salma, Jessa Lynn, Rose, Hunter, Cheyenne, Kat, Sam, Logan, Sammie and Zae—Your honest, detailed, and candid feedback drove me to create the best possible version of this book. Thank you!

To Sarah—For designing the most adorable cover for this book. It was love at first sight and it makes my heart so happy that my readers love it just as much as I do.

To Sandea, Roxan, and Randy—You taught me to believe in myself and to chase my dreams, no matter the cost. I love you always.

To Kyler—Thank you for supporting my insane work schedule while in the midst of moving across the world. Without you my dream of becoming a full-time author wouldn't have come true.

To my ARC team—Even before you saw the cover, read the book, or fell in love with Dawson & Reese's love story, you gave When You Give a Lawyer Kiss a chance. Thank you for all your thoughtful messages, posts, stories, reviews, and comments. Your endless love and support never ceases to amaze me.

Most importantly, thank **YOU**. There are so many incredible books to choose from and I'm honored you took a chance on my story. None of this would be possible without you! Every single tag, share and DM means the world and motivates me to keep writing on the days I think this might be for nothing. I hope you enjoyed your time in NYC with Dawson and Reese.

ABOUT THE AUTHOR

Ann Einerson is the author of imperfect contemporary love stories that will keep you invested until the very last page.

Ann writes dirty-mouthed heroes who love to spoil their women, often fall first, and enjoy going toe-to-toe with their fierce heroines. Each of Ann's books features a found family, an ode to her love of travel, and serves plenty of banter and spice. Her novels are inspired by the ample supply of sticky notes she always has on hand to jot down the stories that live rent-free in her mind.

When she's not writing, Ann enjoys spoiling her chatty pet chickens, listening to her dysfunctional playlists, and going for late-night treadmill runs. She lives in Michigan with her husband.

Keep in Touch with Ann Einerson

Website:
www.anneinerson.com

Newsletter
www.anneinerson.com/newsletter-signup

Instagram
www.instagram.com/authoranneinerson

TikTok
www.tiktok.com/@authoranneinerson

Amazon
www.amazon.com/author/anneinerson

Goodreads
www.goodreads.com/author/show/29752171.Ann_Einerson

Made in the USA
Columbia, SC
25 September 2024

43076196R00155